A
Daily
TRANSFORMATION
THROUGH
"Seasons of Hope"

A
Daily
TRANSFORMATION
THROUGH
"Seasons of Hope"

Mount Moriah Missionary Baptist Church, Inc.

ISBN: 979-8-9989246-3-7

The scriptures in this book were taken from the King James Version (KJV)
– Bible in Public Domain; New International Version (NIV), Holy Bible,
New International Version, NIV Copyright 1973, 1978, 1984, 2011 by
Biblica, English Standard Version (ESV), New Revised Standard Version,
Christian Standard Bible, New King James Version (NKJV), Amplified
Bible, Revised Standard Version, The Message, Contemporary English
Version, American Standard Version, Tyndale Bible, Good News Bible,
New American Bible, The Living Bible, etc. All rights reserved worldwide.

Preface by Minister Dr. Lucretia Wilson

For information on the content of this book,
email: businessoffice@mountmoriahcharleston.com

JMPinckney Publishing Company, LLC
JMPinckneyPublishing@gmail.com

Printed in the United States of America

THE PREFACE

W elcome to the first edition of this Daily Journal, a powerful tool designed to harvest hope and unveil the transformative power of God. By aligning your mind with the truths of God's Word, you will learn to identify and overcome the enemy's distractions, feel empowered to replace negativity with divine truth, and reinforce these insights through biblical principles. The journal is your gateway to new revelations, inspiring the manifestation of miracles, signs, and wonders in your heart. Journaling will provide a safe space of vulnerability to write down your thoughts and feelings and invite later reflections and insight from the Holy Spirit, the ultimate guide in your spiritual journey, who will provide you with the wisdom and understanding you need.

The reflection period compares past challenges or moments to your current life status, which will also impact your future. Embracing intimacy with God will liberate you from sin and pessimistic thoughts, leading you to spiritual enrichment, renewal, growth, and impartation along this journey. As you spend quality time in the Lord's presence, you'll tap into God's secret place, drawing strength from the shadow of the Almighty. His presence will uplift your spirit and fill you with a deep sense of joy and peace, comforting you in times of need.

By dedicating these moments to God, you can cultivate a life filled with hope, peace, and joy in the Holy Spirit. The journey will enable you to discern what is truly good and acceptable in alignment with

God's Word. Embrace core values such as intentionality, integrity, accountability, transparency, consistency, and excellence. These values are the building blocks of a life pleasing to God and fulfilling for you. As you adopt and embody these values, you will feel a deep sense of satisfaction and contentment as your life transforms.

The knowledge and experiences of each writer will guide you toward receiving abundant blessings from God. By casting your cares upon the Lord and leaving them there, you can break free from the shackles and chains that bind you, experiencing a sense of liberation and unburdening. Your personal experiences, when shared in your journal, become a powerful tool that provides both a platform and evidence for making sound judgments and walking in wisdom. Embrace this journey for empowerment to understand the Father's perfect will.

With prayer and purpose,

Minister Dr. Lucretia D. Wilson
Associate Minister
Mount Moriah Missionary Baptist Church

TABLE OF CONTENTS

The Preface v

From The Pastor's Heart viii

January 1

February 20

March 39

April 56

May 76

June 95

July 115

August 134

September 152

October 170

November 189

December 208

Notes: 227

Contributing Authors 234

Mount Moriah Missionary Baptist Church
A Beacon of Hope and Healing 235

Synopsis 237

FROM THE PASTOR'S HEART

Dear Beloved in Christ,

Grace and peace to you in the name of our Lord and Savior Jesus Christ.

It is with deep joy and heartfelt anticipation that I welcome you to this devotional journal— created with love, prayer, and purpose by the associate ministers of Mount Moriah Missionary Baptist Church. This journal is more than a collection of reflections; it is an invitation to slow down, listen deeply, and engage sincerely with the God who meets us in every season of life.

In these pages, you will encounter themes such as hope, love, peace, forgiveness, perseverance, healing, deliverance, and the call to share your gifts with others. Each entry is grounded in Scripture and designed to speak to the real, sometimes messy, always sacred journey of faith. Whether you are going through a storm or standing on the mountaintop, I pray these devotions provide nourishment for your soul and clarity for your path.

As you read, take your time to meditate, reflect, and write. Allow the Holy Spirit to minister to you through every word, and give yourself the freedom to be vulnerable in your journaling. God meets us most powerfully when we approach God with open hearts and honest prayers.

May this journal serve as a companion on your spiritual journey and a testament to how God continues to work in and through your life.

With love and blessings,
In Christ's Service,

Reverend Dr. Byron L. Benton
Senior Pastor
Mount Moriah Missionary Baptist Church

JANUARY

"Surely your goodness and unfailing love will pursue me all the days of my life, and I will live in the house of the Lord forever.'

Psalm 23:6

HOPE AMID UNCERTAINTY

*"For I know the plans I have for you," declares
the Lord, "plans to prosper you and not to harm
you, plans to give you hope and a future."*
Jeremiah 29:11

Life often feels uncertain, and challenges can cloud our vision of the future. Yet, God's promise to us is one of hope—a hope that is steadfast and eternal. His plans for our lives are good, even when we cannot see the complete picture. Hope is the anchor of our soul, keeping us grounded in His promises. Today, rest in the assurance that God's plans for you are filled with His love and kindness.

Reflection Question: In what area of your life do you need to lean into God's hope?

Reverend Dr. Byron L. Benton
Senior Pastor

HOPE

"Blessed are those whose help is the God of Jacob,
whose hope is in the Lord their God."
Psalm 146:5

H ope is not the absence of problems, but rather The presence of God. May you find hope, not because of changing Circumstances, but because JESUS is present In your life.

Reverend Gloria Lightfoot

_____
_____
_____
_____
_____
_____
_____
_____
_____
_____
_____
_____
_____
_____
_____
_____
_____
_____
_____
_____
_____
_____
_____
_____
_____
_____
_____
_____
_____
_____
_____
_____
_____

WHO AM I?

*"Commit thy works unto the LORD, and thy
thoughts shall be established."*
Proverbs 16:3

I often contemplated the question of, who am I or what will become of me? It's taken a lifetime to realize that all of my struggles, secrets and shortcomings were all part of the plan. Nothing comes as a surprise to God. He knows our thoughts before we think them, He knows that wrong turn before we make it, He knows the number of tears that will fall, and He knows our triumphs we will celebrate. Until we acknowledge the gift of God in our lives and that only through and by Him that we live, move and have our beings, we are as a sounding brass; empty and just making noise. How many of us are aware that weeping may endure for a night, but joy comes in the morning? Just know that Spring is Coming! Yet, while it's winter, we must endure the hardship, and plow the fields because when God chooses to use His power to resurrect us or our situations, it doesn't matter how long it has been dead or not working, it will thrive again. Yes, you can flourish and yes, you can prosper, and you can live in the truth of your calling. Just remember to put your trust in God and press forward in faith to overcome obstacles. God is able to put you into positions that you are not eligible for because He doesn't always call the qualified, He qualifies the called.

Minister Sonja Pinckney Rhodes

ANXIETY AMID A GLOBAL CRISIS

"Do not be anxious about anything, but in everything,
by prayer and supplication with thanksgiving, let
your requests be made known to God. [7] And the peace
of God, which surpasses all understanding and will
guard your hearts and minds in Christ Jesus."
Philippians 4:6-7

A nxiety arises from uncertainties, and we are living in unprecedented times. Feelings of restlessness dominate our lives due to ongoing political and health crises. Even in moments of calm, worries about our loved ones demand our attention, making it essential to seek clarity from our leaders. In these times of doubt, trusting God is vital. He invites us to acknowledge Him, assuring us that He will guide our paths. We must seek His presence and burden Him to find true peace. The Word of God asserts that the Lord is near; hence, we should move past anxiety and present our requests through prayer and thanksgiving. Following this guidance, we access peace that guards our hearts and minds. God urges us to stay focused and prayerful in our requests. Trust that He is listening and will make everything beautiful in His perfect timing. Remember, God cares deeply for you and will support you through every challenge.

Minister Dr. Lucretia D. Wilson

5

THE LORD IS THE GIVER AND THE RESTRAINER OF LIFE

"The Lord is my shepherd; I have all that I need. He lets me rest
in green meadows; He leads me beside peaceful streams.
He renews my strength. He guides me along right paths,
bringing honor to His name. Even when I walk through the
darkest valley, I will not be afraid, for you are close beside
me. Your rod and your staff protect and comfort me."
Psalm 23: 1-4

D avid is encouraging us how much our heavenly Father loves us. That He would go the last mile of the way for you and me. He leads, feeds, guides, and shields us. He covers us in any and every confrontation that life throws at us. Through it all, He allow us to rest, He refreshes us, and restores.

Revelation 7:17 For the Lamb on the throne will be their shepherd. He will lead them to springs of life-giving water. And God will wipe every tear from their eyes.

David let us know through the word of God, He will restore our souls. With our souls we process circumstances, we entertain our thoughts, our emotions, and our decisions. Restores means to bring back to its original state of condition, and to make restitution. Jesus is going to restore everything that the devil took.

John 10:10 The thief does not come except to steal, and to kill, and to destroy. I have come that they may have life, and that they may have it more abundantly.

Reverend Graylan Richardson

NEVER ALONE

"I can do all things through Christ who strengthens me."
Phil. 4:13

F eeling all alone? Are you asking yourself "where is God in my suffering? Has He forgotten about me? How will I ever get through these feelings of loneliness and abandonment?"

Is this where you currently stand mentally and emotionally?

Perhaps you are a single parent raising your children alone, you may be a widow who lost a spouse that you have been married to for decades, you may be a young mother who lost a child to death, or perhaps you are a parent who is currently estranged from your adult children, or other family members.

I want to remind you that regardless of how difficult, or how dark the season is that you are currently walking through, God is with you! David reminds us in Psalm 139:7-12 that God is everywhere at once. There is no place that God is not. David mentions some places (heaven, or the depth of the earth) that He thought He could go and God would not be present, but He realized that even in those places God is there.

Today is the day to release yourself from feelings of loneliness and abandonment. A day of new beginnings has arrived for you. Intentionality with purpose must be your goal moving forward. "Immanuel, God with us, is with you" (Is. 7:14, NIV). God's answer to your feelings of loneliness and abandonment is "you are never alone!" "I can do all things through Christ who strengthens me" (Phil. 4:13, (NASB). God bless.

Minister Debra Aiken

_____
_____
_____
_____
_____
_____
_____
_____
_____
_____
_____
_____

IT'S TIME TO WORSHIP

"All the nations you have made shall come and worship
before you, O Lord, and shall glorify your name. For you
are great and do wondrous things; you alone are God."
Psalm 86: 9-10

"**O**h Lord, my God, when I, in awesome wonder Consider all the worlds Thy hands have made." God is so amazing as our Elohim. He made every living creature. He even gave us physical, emotional, and spiritual complexities far beyond human capacity could fully understand. He uniquely designed us so that no one is a true replica of the other. God is a wonder to behold. Let us marvel at His glorious works that He arranges just for us. And I sing, "How Great Thou Art." When we stop and deeply gaze at His beauty and splendor, we connect with Him like no one else can. He uses these moments to draw us closer to Him. In the stillness, He holds us in His arms and refreshes us like the dew on grass early in the mornings. As He embraces us, He takes us to another level in experiencing His love for each of us that is unique. So, I chant "How Great Thou Art." I will trust that You are God. I trust that You know me. I trust that You hear me. I trust You, God. Hallelujah! "Then sings my soul, my Savior God to Thee. How great Thou art, how great Thou art. Then sings my soul, my Savior God to Thee. How great Thou art, how great Thou art." Lift us lift Holy Hands and worship Him.

Minister Dr. Nathalina Rogers-Tolbert

DON'T GAMBLE WITH YOUR SALVATION

"In all your ways acknowledge Him, And He direct your paths."
Proverbs 3:6

Kenny Rogers' "The Gambler" isn't just a song about cards and luck. It's a metaphor for life itself. When we make choices, roll the dice, and hope for the best. But the true gambler isn't the one who risks it all on one hand; it's the one who plays the long game, making calculated moves and learning from every loss.

Like the gambler in the song, we should always trust God, be observant, and having discernment in situations. Do not be like a gambler with your salvation. We must depend on the Holy Spirit to lead and guide us (Proverbs 3:5-6). We should be patient, knowing that the right moment will come. And most importantly, we should always be willing to learn, to take the lessons from our mistakes and use them to improve our future.

So, the next time you're faced with a decision, remember the words of the gambler: "You got to know when to hold them, know when to fold them, know when to walk away, and know when to run."

Minister Rosalyn Brown

THE JOY OF GENEROUS PLANTING

"A farmer who plants only a few seeds will get a small crop.
But the one who plants generously will get a generous crop."
2 Corinthians 9:6

What you harvest in life is directly tied to what you're planting. If your efforts are minimal, so will be your results. But when you sow generously, life responds with abundance. The key isn't just what you give—it's how you give. God loves a cheerful giver because cheerful giving reflects a heart aligned with His. Giving isn't just an action; it's the doing of love. When you give willingly, joyfully, and without reluctance, it's as though your soul joins in the rhythm of heaven. Your giving becomes a blessing not only to others but to you as well. If you're feeling stuck, unfulfilled, or lacking joy, consider this: what are you planting? Are you holding back your time, resources, or love out of fear? Or are you trusting God with open hands, planting seeds of generosity in faith? Remember, giving is the key to joy. It's an act of trust that multiplies the blessings in your life. The more you pour into others, the more God pours into you—pressed down, shaken together, and running over. Today's Challenge: Find one way to give cheerfully today, whether it's your time, your resources, or a word of encouragement. Watch how it fills your heart with joy!

Reverend Randy Adkins, Jr.

WINNING WITHOUT FIGHTING

"This is what the LORD says: Do not be afraid!
Don't be discouraged by this mighty army,
for the battle is not yours, but God's."
2 Chronicles 20:15b

The circumstances of our life may feel overwhelming. The situations may appear too complicated to figure out. It may seem like those against us have all the cards in their hands and we just can't win. Nevertheless, we find hope in these words spoken to King Jehoshaphat reminding us that our position in battle is not always to fight, but rather to witness the glorious works of The One who fights for us.

The people of Judah were in a tough spot. Several of their enemies had formed an alliance to attack them. King Jehoshaphat did not panic or issue a military attack. He sought the Lord through fasting and prayer. This gave Him the strength to openly confess their weakness to the Lord, *"We do not know what to do, but our eyes are on You"* (2 Chron. 20:12).

The people went on in battle prepared not to fight, but to praise and worship God! God then confused the enemy and secured the victory! That day, Our God, Our Deliverer, Our Protector showed us that the one who is with us is greater than the ones against us. We don't always have to fight to win.

Dear Heavenly Father, we place our trust in You. Let no obstacle turn us away from following YOU. You are our Refuge. Our Fortress. Our Deliverer. In You we find rest from our enemies. In Jesus' Name, we have the victory. Amen!
Minister Rhulaunda Donald

_____
_____
_____
_____
_____
_____
_____
_____
_____
_____
_____
_____
_____

THE COURAGE TO FOLLOW

"Jesus said to Him, 'If you want to be perfect, go, sell
your possessions and give to the poor, and you will
have treasure in heaven. Then come, follow me.'"
Matthew 19:21

Sometimes God asks us to release what we cling to the most—not because He wants to take from us, but because He wants to free us. The Rich Young Ruler approached Jesus with eagerness, even kneeling in humility, yet He walked away grieved. Why? Because His heart was more attached to what He owned than to who He could become in Christ.

The courage to follow Jesus requires surrender. Not just of wealth, but of anything that competes with full obedience—our reputation, comfort, control, even our plans. Jesus doesn't just invite us to believe; He invites us to *follow*.

Following may require letting go, but it also guarantees something far more eternal: treasure in heaven and the joy of walking with the Savior.

Ask yourself today: What's keeping me from fully following Jesus? What do I need to release so that my hands are open to receive something greater? Remember, Christ never calls us to give up something unless it is for the sake of something better.

Minister Sonja Pinckney Rhodes

Honoring Dr. Martin Luther King Jr. (Holiday)

*"He has shown you, O mortal, what is good. And what
does the Lord require of you? To act justly, to love
mercy, and to walk humbly with your God."*
Mich 6:8

As we honor the enduring legacy of Martin Luther King Jr., a beacon of justice, equality, and love, we draw inspiration from the profound words of the prophet Micah. In Micah 6:8, we encounter the stirring verse: "He has shown you, O mortal, what is good. And what does the Lord require of you? To act justly, to love mercy, and to walk humbly with your God." This scripture serves as a powerful call to action, urging us to embody justice and compassion in our daily lives.

It encourages us to reflect deeply on our essential role in creating a world where every individual is valued and treated with the inherent dignity they deserve. As we commemorate this significant holiday, let us internalize these principles, allowing them to shape our thoughts and deeds. May we strive to uphold justice, embrace the grace of mercy, and nurture a spirit of humility in our interactions, thereby enriching our communities and fostering a more compassionate society.

Reverend Ocie Gay

WITHOUT JESUS THERE IS NO JUSTICE; NO JUSTICE, NO PEACE

*"To do justice and judgement is more
acceptable to the Lord than sacrifice."*
Proverbs 21:13

Without Jesus, there is no justice, Jesus is in front of us, standing together in unity, to bring salvation to the lost in order to increase the kingdom of God. Trusting in the Lord is to know things will get better. Knowing that inspiration is necessary in order to keep the people engaged and putting the word in their hearts.

When we have compassion for the masses and bring them comfort in all situations, the heart of the people will belong to our Savior Jesus Christ. Taking and sharing the fruits of the spirit will allow us as disciples of Christ to show justice in all we do and reach our destination in eternity where we will be able to rest from our labors and sit and have a little talk with Jesus and tell Him how we made it over.

Reverend Dr. Brenda Joyce Stallings

THE GOLDEN RULE

"Therefore, all things whatsoever ye would that men should do to you, do ye even so to them: for this is the law and the prophets."
Matthew 7:12-KJV

W hat a wonderful world this would be if we treated others as we want to be treated. And how do we want to be treated? Like kings and queens, of course!

Why not choose a person today or tomorrow and treat them exactly as you would want to be treated. You do not have to speak to anyone about this feat. It is better left unsaid. It can be just between you and God. He keeps all secrets.

On the other hand, if you do tell someone about what you are doing, it just might catch on. Pray for the Holy Spirit of the living God to lead you on this mission; for the Holy Spirit leads us and guides us into all truth. John 16:13. This would be a fantastic God move because then they might do the same for someone else, treating people like they, themselves want to be treated, with love, respect, compassion, honesty and grace. Before you know it, your action might start to spread like wildfire! You just might have a group of people treating each other as the Lord prescribed for us in His Word! Loving thy neighbor as thyself. Matthew 22:39.

May the Lord bless you on this journey, my friend!

Reverend Brenda Smalls-Robinson

Who Was Joshua?

"In all thy ways acknowledge Him, and He shall direct thy paths."
Proverbs: 3-6

J oshua was a true man of God and the servant of Moses. Joshua respected God by obeying all His commands. Joshua learned how to be Faithful to God by spending time in the presence of Moses. We are so important to GOD. The day we were conceived in our mother's womb, we were written in GOD'S book.

Our days were ordained by GOD for greatness in the kingdom. **Psalms 139:16**

Take time to ask GOD what I was ordained to do in the Kingdom. Joshua had many assignments in the Kingdom of GOD. During His life, He allowed the spirit of GOD to order His footsteps sometimes, and at other times, the flesh controlled Him. If we walk in the spirit, we will not fulfill the lust of the flesh **Gal. 5:16.**

Successes

- Joshua defeated Amalek with the edge of the sword. **Exodus 17:13**
- Ten spies gave a bad report, Joshua was not afraid of being stoned and gave a good report.
- Joshua didn't ask counsel of the LORD; He made peace with GOD'S enemies! **Joshua 9:14-19**
- Joshua didn't ask counsel of the LORD; He made peace with GOD'S enemies!

So, who was Joshua? He was created from dust like you and me. We are subject to failure without the guidance of the LORD.

Minister Arthur Gaddist

_____
_____
_____
_____
_____
_____
_____
_____
_____
_____

THE GOODNESS OF GOD

"Taste and see that the Lord is good."
Psalm 34:8

T he goodness of God is a profound and unchanging truth that sustains us in every season of life. It is a goodness that is not dependent on our circumstances or our performance, but flows from His very nature. God is always good—whether in times of joy or in moments of trial. His goodness is evident in His love, His mercy, His provision, and His faithfulness to us. Even when we cannot see the way forward, we can trust that His heart toward us is always good.

In the Bible, we are reminded again and again of God's goodness. In Psalm 34:8, we are invited to "taste and see that the Lord is good." His goodness is something we can experience firsthand as we walk in relationship with Him. It is a goodness that meets us where we are, lifts us when we fall, and carries us when we are weary. His goodness does not run out—it is new every morning, always abundant and overflowing.

No matter what you're facing today, remember that God's goodness is with you. He sees you, He knows your heart, and He is always working for your good. His goodness is not just a comfort in hard times, but also a reason to celebrate in every season. So, rejoice in His goodness, lean into His love, and trust that, in every moment, God is good—and His goodness will never fail.

Minister Sonja Pinckney Rhodes

_____
_____
_____
_____
_____
_____
_____
_____
_____
_____
_____
_____
_____
_____
_____

THE LOVE OF CHRIST

"Who shall separate us from the love of Christ? Tribulation
or distress, or famine or nakedness or peril or sword...
As it is written, for thy sake we are killed all the day
long: we are accounted as sheep for the slaughter."
Romans 8:35 - 39

G od is love. HE loved us and HE paid the price for us on Calvary. When you look at Jesus, you see love personified. When you listen to His teachings, you hear love edified. When you respond to His touch, you feel dignified. When you accept Him, you receive love magnified for Jesus Christ Himself, is the very pinnacle, the very apex, the very summit, the very zenith, the very peak, yes, even the very vortex of love. His love exceeds the love that a mother has for her child. His love surpasses the love the newlyweds have for each other. His love transcends the love that children have for their parents, and His love excels the love that the saints even have for one another. Nay, in all these things we are more than conquerors through Him that loved us. For I am persuaded, that neither death, nor life, nor angels, nor principalities, or powers, nor things present, nor things to come, nor height, nor depth, nor any other creature, shall be able to separate us from the love of God, which is in Christ Jesus our Lord.

Reverend Larry Curry

EACH ONE COUNTS

"From Him the whole body, joined and held together
by every supporting ligament, grows and builds
itself up in love, as each part does its work."
Ephesians 4:16

Have you ever observed the individual pieces of fiber in a carpet? Probably not because there does not seem to be much to see. However; if one single piece of fiber begin to unravel, it becomes very noticeable. Not only that but the integrity of the entire carpet changes. It's no longer as strong, and it may even begin to fall apart.

If you pay attention, you will notice that once an individual fiber begins to unravel other fibers follow. Eventually, the entire carpet can fall apart and lose its function. This is what happens in the body of Christ when we are not in our intended position. Each person was created for a purpose and is essential for the body to function properly.

The next time you feel that you do not matter, remember without you, the body would not be as strong or may not function as effectively.

Reverend Valarie Pritchard

FEBRUARY

"May the God of hope fill you with all joy and peace as you trust in Him, so that you may overflow with hope by the power of the Holy Spirit."

Romans 15:13

PRAISE BEFORE THE BREAKTHROUGH

"I will praise the Lord with a song and a thankful heart."
Psalm 69:30

P raise isn't just a post-victory activity. It's an act of faith in the middle of the mess. David chose to praise before the waters receded, and that praise strengthened Him and others.

Journal Prompt: What's one way you can worship God before your situation changes?

Reverend Dr. Byron L. Benton
Senior Pastor

_____
_____
_____
_____
_____
_____
_____
_____
_____
_____
_____
_____
_____
_____
_____
_____
_____
_____
_____
_____
_____
_____
_____
_____
_____
_____
_____
_____
_____
_____

Unfailing Love

"For God so loved the world that He gave His only
begotten Son, that whosoever believeth in Him
should not perish, but have everlasting life."
St. John 3:16

A young woman became pregnant during her teenage years. The child's father, her parents, siblings, the pastor, the church, and the community all rallied around the young parents to provide support. They showed unconditional love and encouragement, helping the young couple complete their education before marriage. This support enabled them to better care for each other and their child. Both parents graduated from college; the young man joined the United States Air Force, while the young woman pursued a career in registered nursing. Nearly 12 years later, they prayed for and were blessed with a daughter. The couple earned their master's and post-doctorate degrees in the medical profession. Their oldest child became an Air Force officer, while their younger daughter became an executive at one of the largest banks in the world. The unwavering love of this family and their community demonstrated that love covers a multitude of sins. Their steadfast devotion reflects our Father God's love when He gave His only Son so that "the world might be saved through Him" (St. John 3:17b, ESV). Are you willing to support your brother or sister in the face of ridicule from the world? Can you set aside selfish motives to uplift your fellow believers in Christ? Selah!

Minister Dr. Lucretia D. Wilson

Happy In Jesus

*"Jesus said to Him, You shall love the Lord your God
with all your heart, with all your soul, and with all your
mind. This is the first and great commandment."*
Matthews 22:37-38

One of my favorite hymns is "Oh how I Love Jesus." It emphasizes a deep and personal connection for me because of what He has done for me. John 4:19 tells us "We love because He first loved us." It speaks to the power of faith and the transformative nature of love. This highlights the importance of finding inner peace and joy through a connection with God. God so loved us that He gave His only begotten Son, that we can have eternal life. It encourages us to embrace our faith journey and to find happiness from within. I Thank you, Father, for Jesus my Savior and Redeemer, who brought me out of darkness to a marvelous light.

Minister Rosalyn Brown

HOPE STILL ARRIVES

"Do not be afraid. I bring you good news that
will cause great joy for all the people."
Luke 2:10

J esus was born during a time when the world felt much like it does today — filled with fear, political corruption, and injustice. The Roman Empire ruled with violence. King Herod, obsessed with power, would order the slaughter of innocent children just to preserve His position. The people lived under heavy taxation and in constant fear. Sound familiar?

And yet... Hope still arrived.

God didn't wait for peace, unity, or compassionate leadership. He came *into* the chaos — not as a warrior king, but as a vulnerable baby in a manger. The Savior was born not in a palace, but in the quiet, forgotten corners of society. His birth was first announced not to rulers or elites, but to shepherds — the "least of these," showing that God's kingdom lifts the humble and overlooked.

In a world teetering on the edge of conflict, where leaders seem to care little for justice or the vulnerable, Jesus' birth reminds us that God is not distant or delayed. He is already working among us — in hidden ways, unexpected places, and humble hearts. So, do not be afraid. Hope is not canceled. Light has not been extinguished. The Prince of Peace still reigns, and His kingdom cannot be shaken.

What "hidden corners" of my life or community might God be using to bring His peace and purpose?

Lord, even in chaos, help me see Your hope. Remind me that You still reign, still move, and still restore – right where I am. I trust You. Amen.

Minister Rhulaunda Donald

ADOPTION

*"The Spirit you received does not make you slaves, so that you
live in fear again; rather, the Spirit you received brought about
your adoption to sonship. And by Him we cry, Abba Father."*
Romans 8:15 NIV

B
e thankful for the option to obey or disobey, to agree or disagree, to believe or not. God does not force anyone to follow Him. Yet, we are taught that the Holy Spirit is gentle and does not enslave anyone. No one is forced to be a believer of Jesus Christ. The believer receives the gift of salvation not to be a slave but to be an adherent or follower of the teachings of Jesus Christ, the Son of God. The Christian lives in reverence to God Almighty. Like salvation, receipt of the Holy Spirit is a gift, which makes your adoption official; signed and sealed.

To call your Creator *Abba* Father is to accept the adoption into the family of deity. Jesus himself died on the cross, was buried, and resurrected on the third day with the keys to hell and death. God's victory instituted the adoption of all those who accept Jesus as Savior and Lord. The adoption entitles Jesus' followers the inheritance of eternity with the Father and the Son. O bless His name! You have been adopted as one of God's very own children. No one can take that from you. Celebrate your adoption. You are part of the most prestigious, royal family ever established.

Dr. Pamela Gay

THE GUIDING LIGHT

"For Your name's sake You will lead me and guide me."
Psalms 31:3

When an author writes a book, they write it knowing what the end of the story is going to be. They know what the end is going to be because they are the creators of the narrative. Did you know that God is the creator of your narrative and has created an awesome outcome for your life because He loves you. As a matter of fact, the Bible tells us in Hebrews 12:2 that God is the Author and finisher of our faith. So, when we are going through dark times, or times of uncertainty or doubt we should look to the light that is Jesus the Christ to guide us toward the great and awesome things that God has for us. The author writes a story already knowing what the outcome is going to be. Likewise God has written our story already knowing the outcome. So why not look to God who will provide all the answers to your questions and will always guide you towards the light that leads to eternal life.

Minister Tristan Simmons

_____
_____
_____
_____
_____
_____
_____
_____
_____
_____
_____
_____
_____
_____
_____
_____
_____
_____
_____
_____
_____
_____

THE GREAT I AM

"And God said unto Moses, I Am That I Am: and He said, Thus shalt thou say unto the children of Israel, I Am hath sent me unto you."
Exodus 3:14

G od is the Great I Am, just as He told Moses that He is, I AM THAT I AM and to say to the children of Israel, I AM has sent me unto you. Again, in the book of John, He says, I Am the way, the truth, and the life; I Am the vine; and before Abraham was, I Am. Then in the book of Revelations, He says, I Am Alpha and Omega, the beginning and the ending, says the Lord, which is. and which was, and which is to come, the Almighty. And He attests that He will give unto Him that is athirst of the fountain of the water of life freely. Therefore, know that you can do all things through Christ who strengthens you when you tap into Him. It is God who puts the desires in your heart and causes you to dream. He has already made a way out of no way, which means if you have faith of a mustard seed, you can have faith to accomplish anything, because all things work together for the good of them who loves the Lord. That is, all that are "the" called according to His purpose. We are because God is!

Minister Sonja Pinckney Rhodes

DON'T WORRY, TAKE IT TO GOD

"God is our refuge and strength, a very present help in trouble.
Therefore, we will not we fear, though the earth be removed,
and though the mountains be carried into the midst of the
sea; Though the waters thereof roar and be troubled, though
the mountains shake with the swelling thereof. Selah."
Psalm 46:1-3

Often times we struggle with burdens that God never intended for us to carry. During these times we must be reminded that we have an ever- present refuge in Jesus Christ. If we were to be notified of an approaching hurricane, tornado, flash flood or mass shooter we would seek refuge.

Likewise, we are in a spiritual battle with a spiritual enemy, therefore we need a spiritual refuge. *"We war not against flesh and blood, "For our struggle is not against flesh and blood, but against the rulers, against the authorities, against the powers of this dark world and against the spiritual forces of evil in the heavenly realms" (Eph. 6.12 NIV).* Jesus has power over all creation and every physical or spiritual being. Therefore, when we become tired and overwhelmed, learn to be still, pray and turn the situation over to God.

Reverend Leonard Bailey

REGRESSION IS NOT AN OPTION

And Jesus said unto Him, **"No man, having put His hand to the plow, and looking back, is fit for the kingdom of God."**
Luke 9:62

In Hebrew and Greek, regression signifies a withdrawal or a return to a previous state. In both natural and spiritual contexts, regression may start on a positive path but can lead to a retreat into a less mature, carnal, and sometimes negative state of being. Avoiding this regression and staying focused on our spiritual journey is crucial. The Gospel of Luke vividly portrays vital events that witness Jesus' unwavering commitment to His journey to the cross. Despite the trials and tribulations, He never wavered; His focus remained steadfast on the mission. We are eternally grateful to God Almighty for His obedience and sacrifice. His unparalleled love for us enabled Him to stay true to His mission, granting us eternal life. Just as Jesus had 'tunnel vision,' my dear sisters and brothers, I believe the Spirit of God is urging us to stay the course! Remember, God's strength and support will sustain you for the journey ahead. Keep your eyes fixed on your mission. He will never abandon you. Therefore, let us remember that regression is not an option but merely a distraction.

My questions are:

1. What steps can you take to avoid regression in your spiritual journey?
2. How can you discern when you are experiencing regression versus healthy growth?

Lastly, in what ways can you emulate Jesus' "tunnel vision" in your daily lives?

Minister Dr. Lucretia D. Wilson

_____
_____
_____
_____
_____
_____
_____
_____
_____

A LOVE RELATIONSHIP

"Jesus replied: "Love the Lord your God with all your
heart and with all your soul and with all your
mind.' [a] 38 This is the first and
greatest commandment."
Matthew 22:37-38

D o you hear what Jesus is saying to you? If you truly love God and your neighbor, you will have no problem keeping this commandment. There is no doubt in looking at Scripture that God's presence and love is real, good, and available to us. Just take a moment to rest in the truth. Then, you can consistently enter into the tangible presence of your heavenly Father's love anywhere and anytime. Have faith today that God created you to experience Him. Encountering His presence and love is made possible entirely by His grace, so it is available apart from any good or bad thing you do. But, know that God will never force His presence or love on you. He only fills up what is open and ready to receive. He sweetly calls you to meet with Him and waits for you to make space in your life to receive what He longs to give: His immeasurable grace, mercy, and love.

The choice is yours. Do not worry about what you should do. Instead, concentrate on all you can do to show your love for God and others. When you obey Jesus, you demonstrate that you trust Him. Obedience is the outward expression of your love for God.

Minister Janet Williams-Johnson

GRIEVING FOR LOVED ONES

"Blessed are those who mourn, For they shall be comforted."
Matthew 5:4

My husband, John, and I had always planned to retire in South Carolina. We envisioned spending our days visiting family, sightseeing, golfing, and staying active in church. At the time, my parents were spiritual leaders at Mount Moriah Missionary Baptist Church in North Charleston, and I was pastoring my second church in Queens, N.Y. We hadn't set a retirement date, but in 2007, the Lord blessed us to purchase a retirement home in Goose Creek, S.C. — paid in full. My parents joined us at the closing, beaming with pride that we wouldn't have a mortgage.

We decided to move to South Carolina in 2015, but none of our plans came to fruition. Shortly after relocating, Mommy became ill and soon transitioned to be with the Lord. I was heartbroken — no more shopping trips to her favorite store, Hamrick's, and so much more. While grieving her loss, my husband John, my rock, transitioned on September 21, 2016. I was devastated. Then, to deepen the pain, my only daughter transitioned on December 23, 2022. Each loss shook me to my core and changed my life forever.

I was comforted by God the Holy Spirit. He put people in my life that prayed with me and walked with me during this grief process. I went to the Grief Share Ministry which helped me tremendously. God's plan includes both sorrows and joys. As a believer, I don't mourn as an unbeliever but I do mourn.

Reverend Dr. Brenda Joyce Stallings

DON'T THINK LIKE THE WORLD

*"For the weapons of our warfare are not carnal, but mighty
through God to the pulling down of strongholds; casting
down imaginations, and every high thing that exalteth
itself against the knowledge of God, and bringing into
captivity every thought to the obedience of Christ."*
2 Corinthians 10:4-5

I f you think like the world thinks, eventually you will act like the world acts. Unrestrained thoughts produce unrestrained actions. So, control your thoughts by bringing them into obedience to the scriptures. Program your mind with the Word of God. The Word is spirit and it is life. When your mind is saturated with the Word of God, your will becomes strong to exercise authority to overcome every ungodly thought and evil habit.

Don't let Satan deceive you into sacrificing the glory of God in your life for a few moments of self-indulgence and sin. Restrain your thought life. Meditate the Word instead of selfish, carnal thoughts. Keep your eyes on Jesus, the author and finisher of your Faith.

Minister Carmen Smalls

IDENTITY IN CHRIST

*"Therefore, if any man be in Christ, He is a new creature: old
things are passed away; behold, all things are become new."*
2 Corinthians 5:17

Your true identity is in Christ; therefore, seek Him deeper, draw nigh unto Him and He will draw nigh unto you. Protect yourself by being vigilantly mindful of your surroundings. Knowing that you will have your confidants; people you can trust and who will support you in sunshine or rain. There will also be your constituents; those who are not for you but for what you are for. They are there to gain what you know and then they will leave you for the next up and coming opportunity. Lastly are your comrades; they are not for you or for what you are for. They are there just to join forces together for what you are against. Again, they will leave you, as well. Make sure you qualify who has access to your destiny.

God doesn't reveal your path to you. He gives you a vision, but not the route. He gives you the dream and, if you're bold enough to chase the dream, He'll get you through the journey. Don't quit in the middle of the journey, God is in the making dreams come true business. Get to know God and you will get to know yourself, and then you can know without a doubt that your true identity is in Christ.

Minister Sonja Pinckney Rhodes

_____
_____
_____
_____
_____
_____
_____
_____
_____
_____
_____
_____
_____
_____
_____
_____
_____

God Knows Your Needs

"Then as He lay and slept under a broom tree, suddenly an angel touched Him, and said to Him, "Arise and eat." Then He looked, and there by His head was a cake baked on coals, and a jar of water. So He ate and drank, and lay down again."
I Kings 19:5-6

In this text, Elijah is coming off His iconic victory against the prophets of Ba'al. God had demonstrated that He was superior to Ba'al by consuming both the altar set up for Him and for Ba'al with fire. It was a decisive victory for the people of God.

Despite that, just a chapter later, things are not going well. He has narrowly escaped King Ahab. He reaches a point of despair so deep that He asks God to take His life. Elijah is allowed to rest under a tree and then is awoken to a meal.

Doing the will of the Lord doesn't guarantee an easy path. But we can find peace in the fact that God knows our limits deeply. We can be honest about our struggles with Him. Furthermore, He knows what we need before we even need it. Ask God to show you His provision in your wilderness. I promise He will provide.

Minister Kon Robinson

WOUNDED PART 1*

"He heals the brokenhearted and binds up their wounds."
Psalm 147:3

Have you ever ached all over, but weren't coughing or sneezing? Had flu-like symptoms, but your nose isn't runny or congested? Didn't have a real appetite and sleep didn't come easy? A general feeling of malaise, but you're not sick physically?

I've had these symptoms. I am sure some of you have experienced them also. I can only explain it by saying my spirit was wounded. What an awful feeling! I can remember missing some prayer times with God. Instead of praying every day, maybe I prayed every other day. Then prayer would be only at meals. Then there was no prayer at mealtimes. Just sit, start eating and talking to each other. Prayer time just seemed to get smaller and smaller until there was none.

Reading the Bible seemed like such a chore. Everything else seemed much more interesting.

Reading billboards, license plates, murder mysteries, romance novels, latest fashion ideas and political news on the internet…etc.

Fellowshipping with other saints at church becomes a drag. Instead, on weekends we make sure to catch the latest movie at the theaters or a baseball game at the neighborhood park.

When we put God and the things of God at the end of our "to do" list, we begin to get spiritually sick. We do not recuperate and begin to get well until we pray and seek the face of God once again.

Reverend Brenda Smalls-Robinson

_____
_____
_____
_____
_____
_____
_____
_____
_____
_____
_____
_____

THE GIFT OF PRESSURE

"Consider it a sheer gift, friends, when tests and
challenges come at you from all sides."
James 1:2

L ife's challenges often feel anything but a gift. Tests are hard, and pressure is uncomfortable. Yet, it's under pressure that the most beautiful diamonds are formed. Your faith-life, refined by trials, reveals its true colors in these moments. The struggles you face aren't permanent—they have an expiration date. But their purpose is eternal. God uses these trials to mature you, to shape you into someone lacking nothing. The hurt, pain, and despair you feel today are the very tools He's using to craft beauty in your life. So, don't rush to escape. Lean into the process. Let the perfect work of God happen in you. Embrace this season, knowing it's not breaking you — it's making you. Your faith is being strengthened, your character is being refined, and your story is becoming one of resilience and glory. Today's Declaration: I declare that these trials are temporary, and God is creating something beautiful in me. I will embrace this moment, trusting in His perfect work. Today's Challenge: Reflect on a current challenge and ask, What is God teaching me? Choose to see this trial as a gift, and let your faith shine like the diamond you are becoming. Start shining!

Reverend Randy Adkins, Jr.

A TIME TO GRIEVE

"Have mercy upon me, O LORD; for I am weak: O
LORD, heal me; for my bones are vexed. My soul is
also sore vexed: But thou, O LORD, how long?"
Psalm 6:2-3

I hope you allow me to walk alongside you through this message of Encouragement during our grief journey. My heart goes out to you. There are no magical words to bring an end to your pain. But I hope the words of this message, will in some small way Comfort, Support, Strengthen, and Encourage you. May God be with you at this time and always.

The most important thought I will share with you is this: **Permit yourself to grieve.** You're human, so let yourself be human. Allowing yourself to **feel** is the best and healthiest thing you can do for yourself and for those you love.

We **ALL** grieve differently, we are uniquely designed by our **Heavenly Father**. When someone dies we have loved deeply, we are left with a grief that can paralyze us emotionally — when they die a part of us dies, too. God never intended us to suffer alone. He created us to care for and support others in their time of need — and to allow others to care for and support us in ours.

> Your tears are the words with which you tell
> God of your pain.
> Be Encouraged in the Lord!

Reverend Gloria Lightfoot

_____

Peace Beyond Understanding

"And the peace of God, which transcends all
understanding, will guard your hearts
and your minds in Christ Jesus."
Philippians 4:7

Peace does not signify the absence of trouble, but rather the presence of God in the midst of it. His peace transcends circumstances, calming life's storms. As you surrender your worries to Him, allow His peace to guard your heart and mind today.

Reflection Question: What do you need to surrender to God to experience His peace?

Reverend Dr. Byron L. Benton
Senior Pastor

MARCH

"And be not conformed to this world: but be ye transformed by the renewing of your mind, that you may prove what is that good, and acceptable and perfect will of God."

Romans 12: 2

THE GIFT OF FORGIVENESS

"Be kind and compassionate to one another,
forgiving each other, just as in Christ
God forgave you."
Ephesians 4:32

F orgiveness is a gift we receive and a gift we give. Just as Christ forgave us, we are called to forgive others. Holding onto unforgiveness weighs us down, but releasing it brings freedom. Today, ask God to help you forgive, even when it feels impossible.

Reflection Question: Who do you need to forgive, and how can you begin that process?

Reverend Dr. Byron L. Benton
Senior Pastor

Devoted To The Deeper Things

"They devoted themselves to the apostles' teaching and to
fellowship, to the breaking of bread and to prayer."
Acts 2:42

D evotion is more than discipline — it's a heart posture. In the early church, believers weren't just participating in activities; they were fully immersed in shared life with God and one another.

This passage paints a picture of people committed to spiritual formation. They studied God's Word together. They didn't just socialize — they fellowshipped, breaking bread with purpose. And they prayed — not occasionally, but as a way of life. The kind of relationship goals we desire — whether in friendships, family, or community, begin with this kind of devotion. When we anchor ourselves in God's truth and walk alongside others who do the same, our relationships are built on something eternal.

Maybe your spirit is craving something deeper. Maybe you're tired of surface-level connections. Acts 2:42 reminds us that the spiritual disciplines we often overlook are the very tools that cultivate lasting relationships. Let this be a week of recommitment. Set aside time for intentional prayer. Share a meal with someone and invite God into the conversation. Read the Word not just for information, but for transformation. Devotion invites the divine.

Minister Sonja Pinckney Rhodes

THE SOVEREIGN PLAN OF RESTORATION

"I am the Lord, and there is no other; apart from me there is no
God. I will strengthen you, though you have not acknowledged me."
Isaiah 45:5

God is not a respecter of person. His divine power allows Him to do whatever and to use whomever. His plans are not confined by human expectations or limitations. Whether we are believers, or not; God rules. Whether we acknowledge Him, or not; He is our Creator. Whether world leaders or local authorities; God is in control. At the time Isaiah delivered the prophecy in chapter 45, the people of Israel - particularly the remnant of Judah - were in a state marked by spiritual decline and looming judgement. Yet, God was already orchestrating a plan to restore them, using a nonbeliever like Cyrus - the pagan King of Persia - to bring about their eventual return and renewal. If God could use Cyrus to accomplish His purposes, then surely He can work even greater things through us when we seek and trust Him.

We can trust God's plan; because even when we don't know the how, we know the Who. So, let us remember Who He is. He is the one crushing the serpent's head. He is the one defeating death. He is the one who restores, confirms, strengthens and establishes us; even when we have suffered for a little while. God has consistently worked towards humanity's restoration, demonstrating His unwavering commitment to our redemption. It is never His intention to harm us, but rather to prosper us. In Him we find hope for tomorrow and eternity. We don't have to fear — we are chosen, called, and empowered to be part of His plan!

Minister Rhulaunda Donald

Spiritual Identity

*"Having predestined us to adoption as sons by Jesus
Christ to Himself, according to the good pleasure of
His will, to the praise of the glory of His grace, by
which He made us accepted in the Beloved."*
Ephesians 1:5-6

W e are not chosen by chance, but by love that surpasses understanding. It whispers of a purpose designed before the foundation of the world. Let us walk in the fullness of this truth, embracing the boundless grace that has called us sons and daughters. For in Him, we find our true identity, and in Him, we are made complete.

Here are some key themes within the passage:

- Divine Selection: We are not chosen by chance, but by a deliberate act of love. This suggests a personal connection with God.
- Predetermined Purpose: Our destiny is not random, but rather, it has been planned before the creation of the world. This implies a sense of meaning and significance in our lives.
- Boundless Grace: We are recipients of undeserved favor. This emphasizes the transformative power of grace and forgiveness.
- True Identity: Our identity is rooted in our relationship with God.
- Completeness in Christ: We find fulfillment and wholeness through our connection with God. This implies that our ultimate purpose is to worship God in spirit and truth.

Minister Rosalyn Brown

THOUGHTS FOR THE JOURNEY

*"Finally, brethren, whatsoever things are true, whatsoever
things are honest, whatsoever things are just, whatsoever
things are pure, whatsoever things are lovely, whatsoever
things are of good report; if there be any virtue, and
if there be any praise, think on these things."*
Philippians 4:8

Our thoughts can determine the direction we travel, the speed at which we travel, and how we perceive the scenery along the way. Thoughts can grow or destroy whatever is conceived in our hearts. Thoughts are like the fuel that empowers a vehicle or can be the accelerant that burns things down when used improperly.

With the destination in mind, thoughts of God's promises, goodness, and faithfulness keeps us and those traveling with us focused, hopeful, excited, and encouraged.

Prayer
Heavenly Father, thank You for Your thoughts towards us and your plans that never change. Keep us reminded and help us to remind others of the expected good end You have planned for us. In Jesus Name, Amen.
Minister Wallace Hunter

A Servant Blessing

"So, He departed from there, and found Elisha the
Son of Shaphat, who was plowing with twelve yokes
of oxen before Him, and He with twelfth. Then Elijah
passed by Him and threw His mantle on Him."
1 Kings 19:19

B eing under the authority of Jesus Christ; there is an anointing and blessings that is attached to it for being one of His servants. Elisha asked Elijah if He could have a double portion of His anointing. Elisha did not receive it until He walked under Elijah's authority for about six to eight years. Walking under the authority of the Shepherd that were place over us is no different than walking under the authority of Jesus.

1 Corinthians 11:1 Imitate me, just as I also imitate Christ. There is a servant blessing, guarantee, even though we go through trials and tribulations, it's only to test our faith and strengthen it.

Hebrews 6:12-15 That ye be not slothful, but followers of them through faith and patience inherit the promises. For when God made a promise to Abraham because He could swear by no one greater, He swore by Himself, saying, "Surely blessing I will bless you, and multiplying I will multiply you." So, after He had patiently endured, He obtained the promise. There is a servant blessing when we obey and follow the man or woman that God has placed us under. The story of Elijah and Elisha is parallel to the story of Jesus Christ and His disciples.

Reverend Graylan Richardson

_____
_____
_____
_____
_____
_____
_____
_____
_____
_____
_____
_____
_____

ANCHORED IN TRUST

*"Trust in the Lord with all your heart and lean not
on your own understanding; in all your ways submit
to Him, and He will make your paths straight."*
Proverbs 3:5-6

Some days carry the heaviness of unmet expectations — the dream that didn't manifest, the prayer that feels unanswered, the opportunity that slipped away. In these moments, it's tempting to question everything. But it's in these very places that trust becomes more than a word — it becomes a lifeline. Proverbs 3 reminds us that trusting God means relinquishing the need to understand. It's choosing to lean into His faithfulness even when the path feels unclear. Disappointment doesn't mean you're off course — it could mean you're being redirected toward something greater. Trusting God with all your heart isn't passive; it's an active surrender of your emotions, ambitions, and assumptions. When we submit our will to God's, He reshapes our journey into something better than we imagined. Your story doesn't end in defeat. Even now, God is straightening your path, clearing unseen obstacles, and crafting a testimony through your trust. He has not forgotten you. Stay anchored.

Dr. Da'rrell Ravenell

_____
_____
_____
_____
_____
_____
_____
_____
_____
_____
_____
_____
_____
_____
_____
_____
_____
_____

NEVER FORSAKEN

"Keep your life free from love of money, and be content with what you have, for He has said, 'I will never leave you nor forsake you."
Hebrews 13:5

G od promises to be with us always. He knew that there would be times in our lives that we would question if we are alone. We might even question if our journey through life is a consequence of our past sins. But God wants to reassure us that He is there even when we can't trace His every move. How can we learn to be content when we don't understand why we are facing our trials? We can remain content when we pray, and when we can remember that God has brought us through our past trials. Those same tests and trials brought us over with a Testimony that it was God that kept us. We should strive to live with our needs rather than chasing our wants. We should appreciate what we have rather than resent what we are missing.

God's love is already expressed in what He has provided. We can take comfort in knowing that Psalm 37:25, says that "I was young and now that I am old" God has never left, or forsaken us. God is immutable and He changes not. Yes there are times when God chastises us, but the consequences are never meant to harm us, but to correct us. Even when God has to correct us, His love is always present. God's love does not abandon His children. As long as Israel was obedient, there was always enough food for everyone. So, we are encouraged to stay obedient and to remain in the will of God.

Reverend Julette M. Scott

_____
_____
_____
_____
_____
_____
_____
_____
_____
_____
_____

BROKEN VESSELS

"And after you have suffered a little while, the God of all grace, who has called you to His eternal glory in Christ, will himself restore, confirm, strengthen, and establish you."
1 Peter 5:10

Why is it that we devalue brokenness? When something is broken, we tend to believe that it has lost its value, that it is useless and needs to be discarded. For some reason we tend to think that it no longer has a purpose. Yet, that is not always true.

In museums, works of art from the past often have more value in their broken state than when they were originally created.

Have you ever considered that your value increases because you have been broken? Every chip that has fallen away tells a valuable story of what you have been through. In the breaking process things have been released, destroyed and removed to shape you into the beautiful master piece designed by the "Master's" hand.

Reverend Valarie Pritchard

TAKING THE INITIATIVE

"And Peter answered Him and said, Lord, if it be thou, bid me come
unto thee on the water. And He said, "Come. And when Peter was
come down out of the ship, He walked on the water, to go to Jesus."
Matthew 14:29

" I am not going to do anything without being told." Many cautious workers have spoken those words. Of all the disciples in the ship, notice that Peter was the only one who took the initiative to converse with Jesus, let alone act. It is easy to play it safe or be cautious; however, as this technological world advances, leaders are looking for workers who will take the initiative. Being a forward-thinker or a Make-It-Happen person is invaluable to any team.

Jesus did not ask if someone wanted to get out the ship and come to Him. Peter said, "If... then." Once the response was given, Peter stepped out and moved forward. Your advancements must be in alignment with the leader. If that leader must tell you every step to take, then that leader might as well do the work. Some workers prefer to ask for forgiveness rather than permission. When the initiative leads to the intended results without causing harm, the worker has simplified or eased the burden of the leader. A leader does not have to do everything. A leader does not have to think for everyone. Take the initiative and step out on faith.

Dr. Pamela Gay

THE COVER-UP

"Therefore, thus says the Lord of GOD of hosts, because you have the spoken this word. Behold, I am making my words in your mouth. Fire and these people would consume them."
Jeremiah 5:14

R omans 3:23 – For all have sinned and come short of the glory of GOD.

Let's talk truth, even since the beginning of time man has desired to do His own WILL and not the WILL of GOD.

Let's talk truth again, GOD created Adam and Eve, He gave them a garden to have dominion over. They could eat and touch anything in the garden EXCEPT the fruit tree in the middle of the garden. It was not GOD'S will, but Adam and Eve ate from the fruit and that is when SIN came in. That is when the **COVER-UP** began then. They said to each other, we better hide and put on fig leaves to hide ourselves (**Gen. 3:3-5**).

Let's talk truth again! What are you covering up? Maybe it's Immorality, Idolatry, and Anger. Are we hiding envy, drunkenness, fornication, adultery, and so much more?

Let's talk truth, Let GOD uncover the **COVER-UP** of sins in your daily lives. **John 1:9** –Confess your sins to GOD.

Let's talk truth again! LORD, Let's ask the LORD to please help me not to be like David by killing Uriah which was a major sin. Uriah was the husband of Bathsheba. He was killed to cover up an adult affair. Remember, that Satan is the master at covering up our sins. He is a deceiver. He will make you believe something that is not true to gain some personal advantages against you and your life.

Evangelist Arthur Gaddist

THE MASTER KEY

"Do not fret because of those who are evil or be envious of
those who do wrong; 2 for like the grass they will soon wither,
like green plants they will soon die away. 3 Trust in
the LORD and do good; dwell in the land and enjoy safe pasture."
Psalm 37:1-3

H ave you not heard that there is a clarion call for the Kingdom of God, the Body of Christ, and the church right now? That is correct! The Lord is calling intercessors, and prayer warriors; "His People" to engage the enemy, the wicked behaviors in the world. This demand may seem out of character to many, yet that time is now.

How are we to do that? I am glad you asked that question. By using the "master key" described in Psalm 37. You and I are asked to:

Trust in the Lord.
Take delight in the Lord.
Commit everything you do to the Lord.

The list continues in this text. Please know that you cannot open a door, if you don't have the correct key. The "master key" is Christ Jesus and the Holy Spirit given to be your guide and comforter.

Minister Janet Williams-Johnson

VICTORY IS MINE

"Praise be to the Lord my Rock, who trains my
hands for war, my fingers for battle."
Psalm 144:1

"When the angel of the Lord appeared to Gideon, He
said, 'The Lord is with you, mighty warrior.'"
Judges 6:12

There is a popular hymn that helps me when I am facing a tough day. It gives me a spirit of tenacity to fight on my knees. This hymn states "O victory in Jesus, my Savior, forever! He sought me and bought me with His redeeming blood; He loved me ere I knew Him, and all my love is due Him. He plunged me to victory beneath the cleansing flood." Hallelujah that we are victorious just because of Jesus. God blessed us that He sent His only begotten Son to die on the cross for our sins, to rise again, and to live forever in Believers. We get to live with power and strength to overcome the snares of the enemy because of Jesus. We get to be vigilant in staying the course from victory just because of Jesus. Yes, we are already victorious because of Christ, and we fight from victory. God has already set the beginning and ending days of our lives. We are fighting the good fight of faith with free will and living out "the dash." So put on the whole armor of God and fight on with the sword in your hand.

Minister Dr. Nathalina Rogers-Tolbert

_____

_____

_____

_____

_____

_____

_____

_____

_____

_____

_____

_____

_____

_____

KINGDOM LANGUAGE

"For at that time, I will change the speech of the peoples
to a pure speech, that all of them may call upon the
name of the Lord and serve Him with one accord."
Zephaniah 3:9

"Bless the Lord, O my soul: And all that is within me, bless His Holy name. *"Bless the Lord, oh my soul, and forget not His benefits* (Psalm 103:2)." Embracing worldly traditions in the Church can be a tempting trap undermining the Lord's work and blessings. Unfortunately, terms like "dope," "lit," and "party" have crept into our conversations about the Kingdom of God. It is crucial to remember that language is a powerful influence that shapes how we understand and express our faith. Instead of adopting these worldly terms, we should treasure the beauty and depth of Biblical language. Think about the uplifting impact of using words like "Holy" and "Righteous" instead of phrases like "Jesus is dope." Embrace statements such as "filled with the Spirit" instead of "let's get lit or crunk for Jesus" and "celebration of faith" instead of "Holy Ghost party." Scripture calls us to *"Praise ye the Lord"* (Psalm 150:1) and *"Let everything that hath breath praise the Lord!"* (v. 6). This is the language that aligns with the Kingdom of God and elevates our worship. So why do we so often blend worldly language with the righteousness of God?

Heavenly language inspires the fulfillment of His promises and supports His mission to restore His people. In Scripture, God uses words that resonate with His purpose and holiness. It's hard to believe that a Holy God endorses language steeped in worldly meanings. Why settle for earthly expressions when the Bible provides powerful promises and benefits connected to our praise? Remember, the choice is yours: embrace the language of the Kingdom!

Minister Dr. Lucretia D. Wilson

_____
_____
_____
_____
_____
_____
_____

WHY DO WE PRAY?

"Is any among you afflicted? Let Him pray."
James 5:13

We pray because it's our way of connecting with God, who loves us and wants to be a part of our lives. Prayer is more than just asking for things we need; it's about building a relationship with our Creator. Just like we talk to friends or family to stay close to them, prayer helps us grow closer to God and strengthen our faith.

When we pray, we can tell God what's on our minds — our hopes, our worries, our joys, and our struggles. God already knows what's in our hearts, but He loves when we come to Him and share. Prayer also helps us focus on what really matters, reminding us that we don't have to handle everything on our own. God is always there, ready to listen and offer His guidance.

Another reason we pray is to ask for help. Life can be difficult, and we all face challenges, but God promises to help us when we ask. Prayer is a way of trusting Him with our problems, knowing that He cares about every detail of our lives. It's also a way to thank God for the good things He's done and to praise Him for who He is.

Ultimately, we pray because it deepens our relationship with God, gives us peace, and reminds us that we're never alone. Prayer is a powerful tool that strengthens our faith and helps us live in line with God's will.

Minister Sonja Pinckney Rhodes

THE FORERUNNER

"John the Baptist Prepares the Way for the Lord, Jesus Christ."
Matthew 3:1-4

I n the above versus of Scripture, we are presented with a very clear and concise description of John the Baptist. In John 1:19-23, the Levites and priests from Jerusalem asked John who He was. In v.23 John simply quoted the prophet Isaiah. "I am the voice of one calling in the wilderness; make straight the way for the Lord." John's message was simple, "Repent, for the kingdom of heaven is at hand."

What does this mean to us? "Get ready, the Lord is soon to return!" Where is the wilderness? The wilderness is places on this earth that are uncultivated and uninhabited where the Word of God needs to be preached and taught. It could be your next-door neighbor or a relative who is uninhabited by the Spirit of God and uncultivated by the teaching and guidance of the Holy Spirit. It is symbolic of people and places where the Word of God is not being spoken and put into effect. John was preparing the way for God's Word. Who is God's Word? God's Word is Jesus Christ. (John 1:1-4)

People must hear the word of God. If preached properly this should lead to repentance. What is repentance? To turn from sin and resolve to reform your life by the power of the Holy Spirit. People's eternal destination is extremely important, and we should be witnesses for Jesus Christ and salvation. Let us begin to evangelize for our Lord by sharing the Gospel of Jesus Christ.

Reverend Brenda Smalls-Robinson

APRIL

"For I know the plans I have for you, declares the Lord, plans to prosper you and not to harm you, plans to give you a hope and a future."

Jeremiah 29:11

Persevering Through Challenges

"Let us not become weary in doing good, for
at the proper time we will reap a
harvest if we do not give up."
Galatians 6:9

Trials challenge our faith, but they also cultivate perseverance. When you feel like giving up, recall God's promise of a harvest. Keep moving forward, trusting that He is working all things together for your good.

Reflection Question: What motivates you to keep going when life feels overwhelming?

Reverend Dr. Byron L. Benton
Senior Pastor

_____

_____

_____

_____

_____

_____

_____

_____

_____

_____

_____

_____

_____

_____

_____

_____

_____

_____

_____

_____

_____

_____

_____

_____

REMEMBER

"I will remember the deeds of the Lord; yes, I will remember your miracles of long ago. I will consider all your works and meditate on all your mighty deeds."
Psalm 77:11 – 12 NIV

Today take time to think about the importance of remembering. This text reminds us to remember. Remember is a phrase that means to bring to mind or think of again. It is a word that can bring up pleasantries and even experiences that we don't want to think about. It is with those memories that we need to remember how God kept you. The Lord has blessed all of us to have amazing memories. Memories with family. Memories with friends. Memories with and about our Mount Moriah church family. Just take time to remember the goodness of God. Remember how God has blessed you. Remember how He brought you this far… thru ups and downs… this and that. Through it all, God has been faithful. God has expressed His love for you through each experience. We are to remember. Remember what Jesus has done for you. Remember what He has said to you. Jesus is saying to you today, "Remember that I love you." Just remember.

Reverend L. Michelle Mitchell

GOD'S LOVE IS WITH YOU

"For I am convinced that neither death nor life, neither angels nor demons, neither the present nor the future, nor any powers, neither height nor depth, nor anything else in all creation will be able to separate us from the love of God that is in Christ Jesus our Lord."
Romans 8:38-39

F or those who might feel a sense of distance from God or who may be unfamiliar with the Church, it's essential to recognize that God's love is both constant and unconditional. This means that no matter our circumstances or life experiences, God's love remains steadfast and ever- present. The book of Romans 8:38-39 beautifully illustrates this point, stating, "For I am convinced that neither death nor life, neither angels nor demons, neither the present nor the future, nor any powers, neither height nor depth, nor anything else in all creation will be able to separate us from the love of God that is in Christ Jesus our Lord."

This powerful message underscores a profound truth: nothing in existence can hinder or sever our connection to God's love. It highlights the idea that regardless of the struggles, doubts, or challenges we face, whether they stem from personal experiences, mistakes, or external circumstances, divine love is always within reach, waiting for us to accept it.

Recognizing this brings reassurance and hope. No matter what your past or present, you are never alone. God's love provides comfort and invites everyone to feel a sense of belonging. This love exists for us without condition, offering peace and encouragement, reminding us that we are valued and cherished just as we are.

Reverend Ocie Gay

THE POWER OF HARMONY

"Live in harmony with each other. Don't be too proud to enjoy the company of ordinary people. And don't think you know it all!"
Romans 12:16

L ife thrives in harmony. The beauty of a symphony lies in how every instrument blends, not in one note overpowering another. Likewise, our relationships should reflect unity, not dissonance. When pride takes center stage, it disrupts the harmony God desires for us to live in. True harmony begins with humility. Treat others the way you want to be treated—with love, respect, and kindness. Resist the temptation to elevate yourself above anyone, regardless of their status. God values every person, and so should we. Wisdom comes not from knowing everything but from recognizing how much we still have to learn. A humble heart, willing to listen and learn, is far more valuable than a mind consumed with its own opinions. To live in harmony, surrender your pride to God, who knows all and sees all. Let His love guide your interactions, and watch how peace begins to flow in your relationships. Harmony is a choice—a daily decision to prioritize love and unity over pride and division. Today's Challenge: Ask yourself: Am I contributing to harmony or dissonance? Commit to treating others with respect and humility, trusting God to bring wisdom and peace into your life.

Reverend Randy Adkins, Jr.

HOLD ON TO YOUR FAITH AND DON'T DOUBT

"This I recall to my mind, therefore have, I hope. It is of the Lord's mercies that we are not consumed because His compassions fail not. They are new every morning: great is thy faithfulness."
Lamentations 3:21-23

"When John, who was in prison, heard about the deeds of the Messiah, He sent His disciples to ask Him, "Are you the one who is to come, or should we expect someone else? Jesus replied, "Go back and report to John what you hear and see: the blind receive sight, the lame walk, those who have leprosy are cleansed, the deaf hear, the dead are raised, and the good news is proclaimed to the poor."
Matthew 11:2-5

There will be times when our circumstances will put our faith to the test. Be encouraged to know that if we belong to Jesus Christ our circumstances are only for a season. God may not give us every detail of His plans and we may not fully understanding why certain things happen.

However, when we start to doubt, remember what we have witnessed Jesus do in our lives. Meditate on God's word, remember where Jesus has brought us from and how Jesus is keeping us right now. God's word and our testimonies will build our faith to have assurance in Jesus Christ.

Reverend Leonard Bailey

HOPE IN THE WAITING

"But they that wait upon the Lord shall renew their strength;
they shall mount up with wings as eagles; they shall run,
and not be weary; and they shall walk, and not faint."
Isaiah 40:31

There is something sacred about the waiting seasons of life. While the world urges us to hurry, God invites us to be still, to listen, and to trust that He is working even in the unseen. Waiting can feel like wandering— uncertain, exhausting, even painful. Yet it is in these quiet spaces that strength is renewed, not lost. When we choose to wait on God, we exchange our fatigue for His endurance, our anxiety for His peace, and our confusion for His clarity.

Consider the eagle. It soars not by flapping wildly, but by waiting for the right current of wind to lift it effortlessly into the sky. That's what hope in God does — it lifts us. Not by our striving, but by His Spirit.

If you find yourself in a season of delay, don't despise it. Lean into the stillness. Let your roots grow deep in faith. Trust that God is shaping you, strengthening you, and preparing you to rise. In the waiting, you are becoming.

Right now, God is not only working on the outcome, He's working on you.

Minister Sonja Pinckney Rhodes

REVIVAL AND RESTORATION

"And they shall rebuild the old ruins, They shall raise
up the former desolations, And they shall repair the
ruined cities, The desolations of many generations."
Isaiah 61:4

R evival and restoration are reminders of how God can work wonders in our lives if we totally commit to Him. They speak to the strength of the human spirit, particularly in times of adversity. The book of Esther is an example of revival, restoration, and being vigilant. Here's a breakdown of the key themes:

❖ Individualism and Solidarity: Emphasizes the importance of standing alone for one's beliefs, even when it's difficult. However, it's not about isolation, but rather about personal responsibility and collective action.

❖ Courage and Resilience: Courage isn't the absence of fear, but the ability to overcome it. It encourages individuals to face challenges head-on, drawing strength from their faith and inner resolve.

❖ Hope for the Future: A sense of optimism and a belief in a brighter future that God will provide. It calls for vigilance and preparation, suggesting that a time of renewal and restoration is on the horizon.

Overall, we must persevere through difficult times, hold onto our faith, and trust in God for a better tomorrow. This is a reminder that even in the darkest moments, He is always with us.

Minister Rosalyn Brown

KINGDOM BUILDING

"But seek ye first the kingdom of God, and His righteousness;
and all these things shall be added unto you."
Matthew 6:33

To understand kingdom building, we must recognize its significance for the people of God. The Kingdom of God is established, but preparation for its rewards is essential. Prayer is a crucial tool, serving as a divine communication channel that empowers and strengthens our connection with God. We can overcome challenges through fasting, prayer, and praise and unlock heavenly blessings. Persistence is also vital; we can intercede for future generations by praying the Word of God and nurturing the seeds we plant, storing up mercy for our families and favor for our children. Proverbs 15:29b reminds us that God hears the prayers of the righteous. In St. Matthew 16:19, during a conversation with Simon Peter, Jesus says, "I will give us the keys of the Kingdom of heaven: and whatsoever thou shalt bind on earth shall be bound in heaven, and whatever you loose on earth shall be loosed in heaven (ESV)." These keys grant us access to deeper revelations through fellowship with Him. To positively influence our daily lives, we must study and apply Scripture. We are responsible for nurturing the seeds we plant for future generations. By committing to these practices, we build for the future and prepare to receive the fullness of God's Kingdom. Let us pray, study the Word, and sing daily, knowing our efforts have lasting impacts.

Minister Dr. Lucretia D. Wilson

GOD REVEALS HIS PLAN

"Then Joseph could not restrain himself before all those who stood by Him, and He cried out, making everyone go out from Him! So, no one stood with Him while Joseph made himself known to His brothers. V2. And He wept aloud, and the Egyptians and the House of Pharaoh heard it. V3. Then Joseph said to His brothers, "I am Joseph; Does my father still live?"
Genesis 45:1-8

So many times, we ask ourselves why. Why is this happening now, what am I doing wrong, what's going on? God has a plan for our lives, it is in His time that He will reveal and show us His plan and why. In John 14:1-14, Jesus tells us that He is the way, the truth, and the life. When we listen and pay attention to the events and things going on around us, God reveals to us what's going on. When we reflect on where we have been and how far God has brought us, He reveals to us what's going on in us and what He is doing through us. In the book of Chronicles, God says that He has a plan for our life, to prosper us and not to harm us, to give us hope and a future. And God will do what He says He will do by any means necessary. He is a promise keeper through trials and tribulations, ups and downs, but the plan is not just about you. Ultimately, it's for His glory and His Kingdom — The Lord sacrificed His Son His only begotten Son that we would not perish but have everlasting life in His kingdom John 3:16. "While we wait, He reveals!"

Reverend Samuel Fennoy

_____

_____

_____

_____

_____

_____

_____

_____

_____

_____

_____

_____

_____

_____

BEARING FRUIT

"Jesus said "I am the vine, and my father is the husbandman. Every branch in me that beareth not fruit He taketh away: and every branch that beareth fruit He purgeth it, that it may bring forth more fruit."
John 15: 1-2

A fruit is a sweet and fresh produce of a tree or other plant that contains seeds. If the fruits fall from the tree to the ground, the seeds from the fruit will then enter into the soil, and will produce more fruit trees. Jesus uses the word fruit as an analogy. As disciples of Jesus Christ, we sow the word of God into individual lives that they may be free from the cares of this world. That they may become productive citizens of the kingdom of God. In the eyes of God, we are fruits in His vineyard.

John 15:7-8" But if you stay in me and obey my commands, you may ask any request you like, and it will be granted!" My true disciples produce bountiful harvest. This brings great glory to My Father.

Reverend Graylan Richardson

BEARING FRUIT IN YOUR LIFE

*"This is to my Father's glory that you bear much
fruit, showing yourselves to be my disciples."*
John 15:8

As believers, one of the most important things we can do in our walk with God is to bear fruit. In John 15:5, Jesus says, *"I am the vine; you are the branches. If you remain in me and I in you, you will bear much fruit; apart from me you can do nothing."* This verse teaches us that as Christians, we are connected to Christ, and through that connection, we are called to produce fruit that reflects His character.

Bearing fruit means showing evidence of the Holy Spirit working in our lives. Galatians 5:22-23 tells us the fruit of the Spirit is *"love, joy, peace, forbearance, kindness, goodness, faithfulness, gentleness and self-control."* These are the qualities that should grow in us as we walk closely with Christ. Just as a tree produces fruit when it is healthy and well-watered, our lives should produce good fruit when we are rooted in God's Word and His love.

However, fruit-bearing isn't just about our personal growth. In John 15:8, Jesus also says, *"This is to my Father's glory, that you bear much fruit, showing yourselves to be my disciples."* When we bear fruit, we glorify God and show others that we belong to Him. This fruit can impact those around us, drawing them closer to God.

Remember, we cannot bear fruit on our own. We must stay connected to Jesus, who is the source of all the strength and grace we need. Let's keep abiding in Him and allow His love to produce good fruit in our lives.

Minister Sonja Pinckney Rhodes

THE SOURCE OF HOPE

"But if we hope for what we do not yet
have, we wait for it patiently."
Romans 8:25

J ESUS is the Greatest source of hope. Our hope is built on nothing less than Jesus blood and righteousness. On Christ the solid rock we stand all other ground is sinking sand. Christ promises us hope not only for Eternity, but also in this life. Keep hope alive.

Reverend Gloria Lightfoot

PERSONAL STORMS

*"These things I have spoken to you, that in Me you may
have peace. In the world you will [a] have tribulation;
but be of good cheer, I have overcome the world."*
John 16:33

J ust as in nature, each of us encounter storms and though they may look different. You may be facing a hurricane that threatens the very foundation of your faith or a blizzard that distorts your vision making it difficult to see what's ahead.

Perhaps, your storm feels like a tornado fueled by anxiety, leaving you confused, twisted by the strong winds of change, and uncertain of your direction. You know the specific of your personal storm, and God knows them too. He sees your struggles but doesn't want you to worry about the storm surge. He has placed you on high ground. Keep your eyes focused on Him, not the rising tide and, He will keep your head above the water.

The storm will cease when you reach out and take hold of the Master of the Wind's hand. When the storm winds cease to blow, you may have lost a few branches, but with a strong foundation, no force will be able to move you — because, the Master has you tethered to His side!

Reverend Valarie Pritchard

RENEWED IN CHRIST

"Create in me a clean heart, O God; and
renew a right spirit within me."
Psalm 51:10

When I consider the term "renewed," words like transformed, changed, and converted come to mind. Have you ever found yourself in situations that don't reflect your identity or beliefs? If so, you're not alone. This is a common human experience. In our scripture, we see King David—a praiser and a man after God's own heart—who strayed from God's will after committing adultery with Bathsheba. He abused His authority, leading Him deeper into sin and despair. However, David eventually cried out to the Lord, asking for mercy, cleansing, and renewal. In verse 10, He pleads, "Create in me a clean heart, O God, and renew a right spirit within me." God, in His loving kindness, restored David. We, too, can seek renewal when we find ourselves in a fallen state or overwhelmed by life's challenges. Remember, God is our transformer. He can turn our wrongs into rights and guide us back to His presence through His Word, renewing us to wholeness. Each of you carries the potential for renewal within you. Stay blessed in the Lord. Remember, God is our transformer. He can change our wrongs to rights and draw us to His presence through His Word to renew us to wholeness. You, each of you, have the potential for renewal within you. Stay blessed in the Lord.

Minister Dr. Lucretia D. Wilson

BEING STILL IN GOD

"Be still, and know that I am God."
Psalm 46:10

L ife can feel overwhelming at times, especially when everything seems to demand our attention — schoolwork, friendships, and even our own thoughts can make us feel like we're always on the go. Sometimes, it feels like there's no time to breathe, let alone find peace. But in moments like these, God invites us to pause and *be still*.

Psalm 46:10 says, *"Be still, and know that I am God."* This simple verse reminds us that God is always present, even when life feels chaotic. Being still doesn't mean doing nothing — it means taking a moment to stop, breathe, and trust that God is in control. It's about choosing to focus on Him instead of letting our worries and to-do lists overwhelm us.

For example, when Sarah, a high school student, felt stressed with her upcoming exams and busy schedule, she decided to set aside time each day to sit quietly and pray. At first, it was hard to quiet her mind, but over time, she began to feel a sense of peace. She realized that no matter what challenges she faced, God was with her, guiding her and giving her strength.

Being still in God helps us remember that we don't have to carry our burdens alone. When we trust Him, we find peace and rest — even in the busiest seasons of life.

Minister Sonja Pinckney Rhodes

The Breaking Point Of Breakthrough

"You will reap a harvest if you do not give up."
Galatians 6:9

B reakthroughs don't usually come when you feel strong. They come when you feel like you have nothing left - when the door slammed shut, when the funds ran out, or the hope started to fade. That's when God steps in and does what only He can do.

When opportunity after another seems to crumble, it can be disheartening. Instead of quitting, choose to keep showing up in faith. Keep praying. Keep praising. Keep declaring God's Word, even when the waiting wears you down. Remind yourself of Psalm 34:17, *that the Lord hears and delivers.* And just when you feel that you have reached your lowest point - when you feel like walking away - it will happen. That's how God works. He often waits until our faith has been tested, until the pressure is highest - so we know the victory didn't come from our own hand.

Why? Because breakthroughs birthed from breaking points carry a different kind of glory. They produce endurance, character, and *unshakeable faith.* God doesn't just want to *give* us the promise - He wants to *prepare* us for it. But you will reap the harvest of the promise at the proper time, if you don't give up during the preparation phase.

So, hold on. If you feel like you've reached your breaking point, lean in closer - because that's usually the place where breakthrough breaks through. Let the rest of your day be filled with expectation — because our God is faithful, and your breakthrough is closer than you think.

Minister Rhulaunda Donald

_____
_____
_____
_____
_____
_____
_____
_____
_____
_____
_____
_____
_____

THE INVITATION

Matthew 11:28

A re you in need of rest for your weary soul? When the cares of this world have overwhelmed you, and you are finding no way of escape from the pain and discouragement life is throwing at you, where do you turn? Or, should I say, whom do you turn to?

Are you in need of true peace? The type of peace that the world, nor things, can give you? If you answered yes to these questions, Jesus is sending you an invitation.

This invite that says "Come to Me" is being sent to ordinary people who are weary and burdened from the cares of this world. The promise for those who come is *"rest for their weary souls* (Matt. 11:28, NASB)."

Unfortunately, many people will not accept this invitation because of pride. Some people prefer to deny or hide the truth about their need for God. If you are willing to be honest with yourself, help is available to you right now from God.

Today, God wants you to exchange your burdens for peace and an eternal assurance of life everlasting with Him.

Are you willing to be honest with yourself and come to Jesus for help? If you accept God's invitation, there is an assurance that Jesus offers to you today. *"Everyone whom the father gives to me will come to me, and I won't send away anyone who comes to me* (Jn. 6:37, CEB)."

Minister Debra Aiken

JESUS FOR JUSTICE, UNITY AND SALVATION

"Behold, how good and pleasant it is for
brethren to dwell together in unity!"
Psalm 133:1

The "U" in Justice stands for Unity. In order for anything to thrive, we need unity. We need to be on one accord following the mandates of our Lord and Savior. Unity is necessary in the body because we can't get along properly without one another. Scripture teaches us all parts of our body are important. For example, we need the ear to hear, the eyes to see. One is not more important than the other.

The "S" in Justice stands for Salvation. Jesus came to save those that are lost. We are to go into the highways and byways and preach the gospel that the wages of sin is death, but the gift of God is eternal life. Salvation is what the world needs now. God's people must live a life that will attract more to the body of Christ. We must treat our neighbors right demonstrating the fruits of the spirit, Love, Joy, Peace, Patience, Kindness, Goodness, Faithfulness, Gentleness, and Self-Control. *"And Moses said to the people," Do not be afraid. Standstill, and see the salvation of the Lord, which He will accomplish for you today. For the Egyptians whom you see today, you shall see again no more forever."* (Exodus 14:13).

Reverend Dr. Brenda Joyce Stallings

HEALING FOR THE BROKEN

"He heals the brokenhearted and binds up their wounds."
Psalm 147:3

G od is our healer, mending the broken pieces of our hearts and lives. Whether your wounds are physical, emotional, or spiritual, God's power is more than enough. Invite Him into your pain and allow His healing touch to restore you.

Reflection Question: What area of your life needs God's healing today?

Reverend Dr. Byron L. Benton
Senior Pastor

MAY

"May the God of hope fill you with all joy and peace as you trust in Him, so that you may overflow with hope by the power of the Holy Spirit."

Romans 15:3

FREEDOM FROM THE TRAP OF PEOPLE-PLEASING

"If possible, live peaceably with all."
Romans 12:18

You cannot please everyone, and you do not have to. When you let go of needing others' approval and rest in God's acceptance, you walk in freedom. The mud of rejection cannot stick when you are covered in grace.

Journal Prompt: Whose approval have you been chasing? What would it look like to release that today?

Reverend Dr. Byron L. Benton
Senior Pastor

_____
_____
_____
_____
_____
_____
_____
_____
_____
_____
_____
_____
_____
_____
_____
_____
_____
_____
_____
_____
_____
_____
_____
_____
_____
_____

LIVING STONES

"Jesus declares that He will build His church upon the rock of
Peter's confession, and the gates of hell will not prevail against it."
Matthew 16:18

I t is not the stones and the mortar, ordinances or rituals that create the church. The church is built on a foundation of faith. That foundation is Jesus Christ. Isaiah (28:16). Calls Him the Cornerstone. 1 Peter 2:5 describes the believers as living stones to be used by God to create a spiritual temple. When we gather together the invisible becomes visible and the kingdom of God is revealed, a place where miracles, signs and wonders take place and the Gospel of Jesus Christ is preached worldwide. The living stones that are laid must be interlocked. In this manner, they provide strength and stability, and the gates of hell will not prevail against it. Matthew 16:18

Reverend Thomas Robinson, Sr.

EXCERPTS FROM "FRESH AIR" LOVE

*"A new commandment I give to you, that you love one another,
even as I have loved you, that you also love one another."*
John 13:34

J esus gives us a simple yet profound command: *"A new commandment I give to you, that you love one another, even as I have loved you, that you also love one another."* Unlike Moses, who gave over 600 commandments, Jesus boiled it down to one — love.

This love is the very love Christ has shown us: selfless, unconditional, and sacrificial. He loved us when we were unworthy, and He calls us to love others in the same way. Loving others as Christ loved us means showing kindness, patience, and forgiveness, even when it's difficult.

Let us take this command seriously and strive to love others the way Jesus loves us. It's through this love that we reflect Christ's character and truly follow Him.

Until tomorrow, beloved, let's commit to loving one another with the love of Christ.

Reverend Brenda Smalls-Robinson

You Are The Salt

"Ye are the salt of the earth: but if the salt have lost
its savor, wherewith shall it be salted?"
Matthew 5: 13

Ye are the salt of the earth: but if the salt have lost its savor, wherewith shall it be salted? It is thenceforth good for nothing, but to be cast out, and to be trodden under foot of men. Salt in this passage, is synonymous to the goodness of God. O taste and see that the Lord is good. Blessed is the man that trusts in Him. But how can we be salt of the earth if we don't allow the Lord to shake us; and if we continuously allow the enemy to keep us entrapped?

It is so easy to get caught up and distracted with the things of this world that shakes our spirits. We can be shaken with fear, but remember, God has not given us the spirit of fear but of love, power and of a sound mind. We can be shaken with deficiencies, but God's word says, He will supply all of our needs according to His riches in Glory. We can also be shaken with guilt, but the book of Romans says, there is therefore now no condemnation to them which are in Christ Jesus.

God shakes us, because there is something on the inside that needs to come out to affect others. Just as seasoning has no flavor, it therefore has no value. Christians should not blend with the world; we should have the flavor of God in everything we do to bring out the God-flavors of this earth.

Minister Sonja Pinckney Rhodes

Yes, There Is Hope

"May the God of hope fill you with all joy and peace in believing,
so that by the power of the Holy Spirit you may abound in hope."
Romans 15:13

A ccording to Merri and Webster's Dictionary, hope is something a person wants to happen. Placing our hope in God helps us trust His promises. Be encouraged to have hope only in the Lord. The great hymn, My Hope Is Built, helps us to be resilient. The first verse is so powerful and gives conviction that "My hope is built on nothing less Than Jesus' blood and righteousness. I dare not trust the sweetest frame But wholly lean on Jesus' name. On Christ the solid rock I stand, All other ground is sinking sand. This hymn reminds us to place our hope in a person who will never fail us. He is omnipresent and omniscient. And when we hope in the Sovereign God, the one who is in control of all things, it gives us peace of mind. Hope helps you to see beyond the present situation. Hope becomes a driving force of tenacity and strength to push us to endure the uncomfortable season. So, rest knowing where your hope lies- in Jesus.

Minister Dr. Nathalina Rogers-Tolbert

JESUS FOR JUSTICE, TRUST AND INSPIRATION

*"Trust in the Lord, and do good. Dwell in the
land, and feed on His faithfulness."*
Psalm 37:3

The "T" in Justice stands for trust. Trust in the Lord with all your heart and lean not to your own understanding. If we trusted the Lord, there would be no uneasiness about following directions during the Pandemic like taking the Covid-19 vaccine, masking up for our protection and people around us. Millions of people died across all nations due to this disease. However, the Lord made a way for the vaccine to be formulated. So why were there people who did not comply?

The "I" in Justice stands for inspiration. In order to fight Covid-19, we had to go into isolation to stop the spread of the disease. We felt lonely, lost, unloved, uncomfortable and unhappy. We were not used to spending time with our immediate household with little distractions. Abusive behavior began to be commonplace in some households. Why? Jesus was not part of the everyday life. "All scripture is given by inspiration of God and is profitable for doctrine, for reproof, for correction, for instruction in righteousness, that the man of God may be complete, thoroughly equipped for every good work." (2 Timothy 3:16, 17)

Reverend Dr. Brenda Joyce Stallings

Cut But Not Cut-Off

"I am the true vine, and my Father is the gardener. He cuts off
every branch in me that bears no fruit, while every branch that
does bear fruit He prunes so that it will be even more fruitful."
John 15:1-2

Jesus gives His disciples a lesson about fruit-bearing. The characters are God the Father as the gardener, Jesus the Son of God as the true vine, and the believer as the branch. The fruit-bearing process is two-fold. Firstly, the believer must submit or humble oneself to pruning by the Father. The Gardener checks your connection for life, growth, and renewal. The Divine Gardener cut away parts of the branches that die or rot, including carefully treating any diseases.

Secondly, the believer must abide or remain actively in existence in the True Vine. Apart from Him, the believer/branch dies. The vine is believer's most nutritious source and life-giver for growth and producing fruit. To remain rooted in the Son, the believers submit to the love and obedience that Jesus modeled.

The successful results are abundant fruit and glorification for the Father. The gardener enjoys seeing the abundant growth and display of transformation of the branches due to connectivity to the true vine.

The believers produce fruit in the kingdom! Yes, the Gardener cuts or prunes, but you are not cut off from the source. Things that are not like God are pruned so that believers can blossom. What can use some pruning from your life?

Dr. Pamela Gay

_____

_____

_____

_____

_____

_____

_____

_____

_____

_____

_____

_____

_____

SECRETS OF THE HEART

"Trust in Him always, ye people pour out your heart before Him: God is a refuge for us."
Psalms 62:8

Abraham had a secret of the heart; He loved Sarah with all His heart. He wanted to bless her with a child but knew it was physically impossible because He was 100 years old, and Sarah was 90 years old. Abraham knew that with God, all things are possible because we serve an omnipresent, omniscient God who made Heaven and Earth. Abraham remembers that God changed Sarai's name to Sarah, meaning a Mother of Nations and Kings of people shall come from her. During that time God promises to Bless Sarah with a Son (Gen. 17:15-16).

Faith is a powerful spirit of God, if we as Christians allow it to dictate our lives. Abraham being 100 years old, didn't walk in disbelief when God told Him that Sarah His wife would conceive a child in her womb at an old age (Rom. 4:20-22).

Abraham is known as the Father of Faith. We as His children must not waver in unbelief. The word of God states: Without faith, it is impossible to please Him: For it is impossible to please Him. For He that cometh to God must believe that He is and that He is a rewarder of them that diligently seek Him (Heb. 11:6). Remember that Hannah had a secret of the heart, she was married to Elkanah who had another wife named Peninnah with children, yet Hannah had no children. Peninnah would always provoke her so much that she would cry and not eat. Hannah went to the temple and poured out her heart to God. God granted her a petition with a Son named Samuel. Remember, if you have a secret of the heart, tell it to JESUS. *"The sacrifice of the wicked is an abomination to the Lord: but the Prayer of the upright is His delight* (Prov. 15:8)."

Evangelist Arthur Gaddist

_____
_____
_____
_____
_____
_____
_____
_____

GOD IS OUR REFUGE

"The Lord is good, a strong refuge when trouble comes."
Nahum 1:7

The goodness of God is a constant, unshakable truth that we can rely on in every season of life. It is a goodness that is not defined by our circumstances but by God's unchanging nature. No matter what happens around us, His goodness remains steady, faithful, and abundant. Psalm 34:8 invites us to "taste and see that the Lord is good." It's an invitation to experience His goodness for ourselves — every day, in every moment.

God's goodness is evident in the way He loves us, cares for us, and provides for us. Even when we don't see it or understand it, He is working behind the scenes, orchestrating His perfect plan for our lives. His goodness is not based on what we deserve, but on His grace, mercy, and compassion. It is a love that never falters, no matter how often we stumble.

When life feels uncertain or difficult, remember that God's goodness is a firm foundation you can stand on. His promises are true, and He will never abandon you. Even in times of hardship, His goodness works in us and through us, bringing healing, strength, and purpose.

The goodness of God calls us to respond with gratitude and trust. When we recognize His goodness, our hearts overflow with worship, knowing that no matter what life brings, He is always good. Take a moment today to reflect on His goodness, and let it fill you with peace, hope, and joy. You are loved by a good and faithful God.

Minister Sonja Pinckney Rhodes

Perfect Love Casts Out Fear

"There is no fear in love; but perfect love casteth out fear."
1 John 4:18

Fear paralyzes. It whispers doubts, raises walls, and keeps you stuck in a cycle of "what ifs." But love? Love is fearless. It drives action, breaks down barriers, and sets you free. God's perfect love doesn't just coexist with fear—it pushes it out entirely. The love of God isn't abstract; it's tangible. It's Jesus stepping into our brokenness, His arms stretched wide on the cross, declaring, "You are worth it." That same love lives in you. It's the kind of love that inspires boldness, kindness, and faith, even in the face of uncertainty. When you embrace God's love, fear loses its grip. You stop worrying about rejection because you know you are accepted. You stop hesitating to act because His love compels you to move. But love doesn't stop with you. It's meant to flow through you. Make love tangible today—reach out to someone in need, forgive where it's hard, or speak life into someone who feels unseen. Today's Declaration: I declare that fear has no place in my life because I am fully loved by God. His perfect love fills me, drives me, and pushes fear out. Today's Challenge: Ask God to show you one way to make His love tangible to someone else. Watch how love not only transforms them but also sets your own heart free.

Reverend Randy Adkins Jr.

THE ACTIVE LISTENER

"Ask and it will be given to you; seek and you will find;
knock and the door will be opened to you. [8] For everyone
who asks receives; the one who seeks finds; and to
the one who knocks, the door will be opened."
Matthew 7:7-8

H ave you ever been in a conversation with someone where you were expressing yourself to them about something that was important to you, only to find out they were never really listening to anything you said? What a frustrating experience when you have poured your heart out to someone, hoping that they will give you support only to find out that their body was there, but their mind was somewhere else. Communication is a key factor in forming strong relationships. It is important that others understand us when we talk and equally important that we offer others the same. For one reason or another though there are times when we don't give our full attention to the matter at hand. God is always ready to listen to what we have to say, and always ready to give an answer. God hears us when we talk, and He always gives the perfect response to what we are seeking. When we have questions that need answering, or petitions that need to be addressed, let us look to God who will give us what we ask for, help us find what we are seeking, and open every door that we knock on according to His will.

Minister Tristan Simmons

Unwavering Faith

"Now faith is the substance of things hoped
for, the evidence of things not seen."
Hebrews 11:1

The story of Daniel and His friends in Babylon is a powerful example of unwavering faith. They remained steadfast in their belief in God even when faced with immense pressure and temptation. Their story is a reminder that with God's strength, we can overcome any challenge and remain faithful to our convictions. On this Pilgrim journey, we will at one time or another have our faith tested. The way we handle life's trials and tribulations depends solely on our faith in God (Romans 10:17). Our spiritual survival and faith depend on these important factors:

- Relationship with God
- Studying the word of God
- Being obedient to God
- Having strong prayer life

We must develop a vertical and personal relationship with God, and have a transformed mind with things eternal. We must know the word, whose we are, and whom we serve especially in the time of trouble, so that we can rely on our faith in God to get us through just as He helped Daniel and His friends with their unwavering faith.

Minister Rosalyn Brown

BEYOND CHARIOTS

"Some trust in chariots and some in horses, but
we trust in the name of the Lord our God."
Psalm 20:7

I n the ancient Near East, chariots and horses were the cutting edge of military technology. They represented not only physical strength and speed but also the wealth and resources of a nation. Kings and armies relied on these for swift maneuvers and decisive victories in battle.

In modern America, many look to government, military, technology, and economic systems - the "chariots and horses" of our time - for security and progress. Yet, like their ancient counterparts, these systems have limitations and can fail or falter under pressure. True security comes from trusting in the name of the LORD — a trust that is not limited by the constraints of human effort. No matter how impressive human resources may seem, they pale in comparison to God's ability to save and restore.

Our security isn't found in the power of technology, money, or political clout, but in the unshakeable, sovereign rule of God. True and lasting victory comes only through reliance on God's strength and intervention. Despite the uncertainty of times, we serve a certain God. His sovereign power is greater than human strength.

Dear Lord, You are a Mighty Deliverer. A Sovereign Redeemer. Forgive us for falling short to fully rely on You. May You be our rock, fortress, and deliverer; our God and strength in whom we take refuge. In Jesus Name, Amen.

Minister Rhulaunda Donald

ONE SOUND, ONE BAND

"I want to plant seeds of peace and prosperity among you."
Zechariah 8:12

W hen you are in harmony with the Lord, then you can take heart and finish the task assigned to your life. What task? Whatever God placed in your hands to complete for the Kingdom of God. You see, when you receive the word of God outlined from His prophets, teachers, and preachers, you are ready to work. All you need is to take it to heart and do what God want you to do.

Plant those seeds of peace which is freedom from disturbance; tranquility and prosperity flowing in successful, flourishing, or thriving condition. God is calling you to harmony with Him. This is how you begin the work in your personal life resulting in "one sound and one band" for God. These harvests will produce grapevines that are so heavy with fruits. Don't be afraid of what you see today.

This is not all of it. God wants to make you a symbol and source of blessing. But you must trust and rebuild individual temples for God.

Minister Janet Williams-Johnson

THE GIFT OF WORSHIP IN SONG

"For the gifts and calling of God are without repentance."
Romans 11:20

T he gift of song and the calling of God are eternal and without regret. But how can we genuinely worship in song and spirit in a strange land? Will burdens be lifted, hearts made whole, and souls released from their chains? Or will feelings stem from our talents? The question arises: how can we discern genuine worship from mere performance? We must consider the distractions that might divert us from our divine purpose. True worship should edify God's church, not serve our glory. As Psalmists of the Gospel, we must invite the Spirit of God to purify our hearts and cleanse us from worldly distractions. The gift of song is meant for God's glory— who can ascend the Holy Hill of God? The answer lies in having clean hands and a pure heart. We must carry the mantle of worship with humility and selflessness, recognizing that we cannot serve the world and the Lord. If we love the gift but neglect our calling, we miss the point. Disciples chosen by God focused singularly on their mission, rejecting worldly pleasures for divine purpose. So, my sisters and brothers, what is the Holy Spirit nudging you to let go of today? Remember, the Holy Spirit desires to transform you into the vessel and worshiper He needs. Fully commit to Him and His will today!

Minister Dr. Lucretia D. Wilson

_____
_____
_____
_____
_____
_____
_____
_____
_____
_____
_____
_____
_____
_____
_____

MEMORIAL DAY
COMFORT AND HOPE

"The Lord is close to the brokenhearted and
saves those who are crushed in spirit."
Psalm 34:18

T o the families who have endured the immense sorrow of losing their loved ones, we sincerely extend our deepest condolences. As you navigate through this incredibly challenging period, please know that you are in our thoughts and prayers. Although words may seem inadequate in expressing the depth of your pain, we hope you can find some solace in the knowledge that you are not alone. There is a divine presence, a source of comfort and strength, watching over you and enveloping you in love. The poignant words, "The Lord is close to the brokenhearted and saves those who are crushed in spirit," carry profound significance in times like these. They acknowledge the weight of your grief and offer a message of hope and comfort to guide you through the darkness. This message reminds you that you are not alone in your sorrow.

We recognize the sacrifices made by you and your loved ones and honor their memory with deep respect. Please remember that you are not alone in your grief. You have a network of support surrounding you, ready to stand by your side with unwavering compassion and solidarity. Lean on those who care for you and allow their love to uplift you as you continue to heal.

Reverend Ocie Gay
U.S Army Retired
Purple Heart Recipient

GREATER WORKS

"Verily, verily, I say unto you, He that believeth on me,
the works that I do shall He do also; and greater works
than these shall He do; because I go unto my Father."
John 14:12

J esus promises in John 14:12, *"Very truly I tell you, whoever believes in me will do the works I have been doing, and they will do even greater things than these, because I am going to the Father."* This verse is powerful—it tells us that as believers in Christ, we are called to do *greater works* than Jesus Himself did during His time on earth. But what does that mean, and how can we live it out?

First, it's important to understand that "greater works" isn't about doing bigger or more impressive things. It's about the impact we can have through the power of the Holy Spirit. Jesus' ministry was amazing—He healed the sick, performed miracles, and preached the gospel. But after He returned to the Father, He sent the Holy Spirit to live inside of us. The Holy Spirit empowers us to continue Jesus' mission in the world.

Through the Holy Spirit, we are equipped to do things that carry the message of God's love and salvation to those around us. Whether it's helping others, sharing the gospel, or showing kindness and compassion, these are the "greater works" Jesus is talking about. As the body of Christ, we are His hands and feet on earth, and He works through us to bring hope to a broken world.

Remember, these greater works are possible not because of our own strength, but because of the Holy Spirit working in us. We can trust that God will use us to do amazing things for His kingdom!

Minister Sonja Pinckney Rhodes

_____
_____
_____
_____
_____
_____
_____
_____
_____
_____
_____

DON'T RENEGE ON YOUR COVENANT

"Now when He had finished speaking to Saul, the soul of Johnathan was knit to the soul of David, and Johnathan loved Him as His own soul. Then Johnathan and David made a covenant because He loved Him as His own soul."
1 Samuel, 18:1, 3

A covenant is a relationship between two partners who make binding promises to each other, and is accompanied by an oath, sign or ceremonies. When two people get married they enter into a covenant with one another. What happens if one reneges on the vows? Serious consequence could happen. In 1st Samuel, Johnathan had loved David as His own soul. The covenant between Johnathan and David, pictures a covenant that the Christians have with Jesus Christ. We believe that there is life after death and there is one of two places one would spend eternity, which is heaven or hell, and Jesus is the only one who can get us to that glorious place called heaven.

Romans 10:9 *"That if you confess with your mouth the Lord Jesus and believe in your heart that God raised Him from the dead, you will be saved."* We have a covenant with Jesus; He is the only one; wherefore, one can be forgiven of their sin and be reconciled with God. He is the mediator between God and humanity.

John 3:16 *"For God so loved the world that He gave His only begotten Son, that whosoever believes in Him should not perish but have everlasting life."*

Reverend Graylan Richardson

JUNE

"Fear not, for I am with you; be not dismayed, for I am your God; I will strengthen you, I will help you, I will uphold you with my righteous right hand."

Isaiah 41:10

DELIVERANCE THROUGH CHRIST

"The righteous cry out, and the Lord hears them;
He delivers them from all their troubles."
Psalm 34:17

God is our deliverer, faithful in rescuing us from sin, fear, and bondage. When we cry out to Him, He hears us and responds. Trust in His ability to set you free and walk boldly in the freedom He provides.

Reflection Question: Where in your life do you need God's deliverance?

Reverend Dr. Byron L. Benton
Senior Pastor

THE POWER OF SHARED GENEROSITY

"All the believers were together and had everything in common."
Acts 2:44

R eal love is generous. Not just with things — but with time, patience, compassion, and resources. The early church had a spirit of radical generosity that wasn't about obligation, but about love. They gave because they saw their blessings as a means to bless others. In a world that often teaches us to protect what's ours, Scripture teaches us the opposite: *hold loosely, share freely, and trust God to supply all your needs.*

Generosity reflects the heart of Christ. When we give without fear, we mirror the One who gave everything. The early believers didn't just give; they *saw* each other's needs. That kind of community requires attentiveness. Who around you might be quietly struggling? Who might need a listening ear, a meal, or even a financial lift?

Our possessions are tools — not trophies. And our love, when expressed through giving, becomes a testimony of the gospel. As you reflect today, consider how generosity shows up in your relationships. Ask God to show you new ways to give, not out of pressure, but from a heart of love and trust. The blessing you give always multiplies in His hands.

Minister Sonja Pinckney Rhodes

No Looking Back

But Jesus told Him, "Anyone who puts a hand to the plow
and then looks back is not fit for the Kingdom of God."
Luke 9:62 NLT

G rowing in your discipleship requires focus. Focus on developing your relationship with our Lord Jesus Christ. It requires being available to Him. It requires attention to what God has ahead of you. When you commit to a relationship with Jesus, you must always be determined to look forward. During the writing of Luke 9, plows were very different than the ones today. Because of the plow's design, the one using the plow had to be focused. Also, the person had to keep their hand on the plow, or it would tip over or go off to the side. The person had to focus on the direction they were going and the speed of the animal pulling the plow. Plowing means to turn over. It means to till and to be worked. Plowing uses what is already there to stir up and enrich. Using the soil, the stones, whatever is in the ground, and stirring it up. You must be willing to let God till you as a field. He wants to continue to grow you. He wants to tend to your soil by turning it, breaking up those hard, stony places, and enriching it with His Word. You have to hold on and let God stir you! Keep going forward with your eyes on Jesus because He is your hope. Keep pressing on! There's no looking back!

Reverend L. Michelle Mitchell

OPEN BOOK TEST

*"I call heaven and earth to record this day against you, that
I have set before you life and death, blessing and cursing:
therefore, choose life, that both thou and thy seed may live."*
Deuteronomy 30:19

I n this life we'll have many tests and on our journeys we'll have many turns and choices to make. God, our Creator, designed us to past the test and reach the ordained destination. So much so that He gave us His Word filled with answers and Promises. Let it be the GPS (God's Planned Success) that guides your choices.

Minister Wallace Hunter

FAITHFULNESS

"This I recall to my mind, therefore have, I hope. It is of the Lord's
mercies that we are not consumed because His compassions fail
not. They are new every morning: great is thy faithfulness."
Lamentations 3:21-23

We encounter a heartfelt description of God's goodness in the song "Faithfulness of God" by CeCe Winans. He is indeed good, but faithfulness is also one of His defining attributes. God's faithfulness fosters a sense of entitlement among His children — not based on our actions, but on His compassionate love for us. Privilege in our relationship with the Heavenly Father is rooted in our obedience and how we fulfill our purpose. It's important to clarify: this entitlement is not a result of being spoiled in the way we may perceive from earthly parents. The Scriptures urge us to be steadfast, unmovable and always abounding in the work of the Lord. When we diligently pursue our calling and assignment from God, seeking His Kingdom and righteousness first, benefits naturally follow. As the Word states, these benefits entitle us. God rewards those diligently seeking Him, honoring our obedience above mere sacrifices. It's not just about our faithfulness; it's about His unwavering faithfulness to His children. Great is Thy faithfulness! He grants us new mercies every morning.

Minister Dr. Lucretia D. Wilson

WHEN JESUS SHOWS UP

*"In the past God spoke to our ancestors through the prophets at
many times and in various ways, but in these last days He has
spoken to us by His Son, whom He appointed heir of all things, and
through whom also He made the universe. The Son is the radiance
of God's glory and the exact representation of His being, sustaining
all things by His powerful word. After He had provided purification
for sins, He sat down at the right hand of the Majesty in heaven."*
Hebrews 1:1-3

It's important to understand that Jesus created and sustains all things
(John 1:3). In the beginning, when this earth was without form and
void, it was Jesus who showed up and called everything that exist into
order (Gen. 1).

Jesus is eternal and stepped down from eternity to be born as a man.
He showed up as our Savior and sacrificed himself on the cross. He paid
the price for our sins, once and once He made purification for sin He sat
down. Jesus sitting down, symbolizes that the work for salvation was
finished. When Jesus shows up at His second coming all that He has
promised shall be fulfilled.

Reverend Leonard Bailey

CAST YOUR CARES UPON THE LORD

"Cast your cares upon Him for He cares for you."
1 Peter 5:7

God, who is the creator of the universe and all creation, cares deeply about you and me.

Are you currently feeling burdened and heavy-laden? If you answered 'yes' to this question, I have some good news for you. Today, God wants you to *"cast your cares upon Him, for He cares for you* (1 Pet. 5:7, NIV)." The word 'cast' means to throw off. Jesus is telling you to throw off every burden, hindrances, anxiety, worry or fear that may be holding you captive in your mind, even now.

Are you tired of carrying your heavy loads called worry, fear, anxiety, and stress? Will you release it to God right now? He is willing to carry it for you. God is the one you can trust with all your cares. God calls you friend.

Do you hear God speaking to you as you read this journal? I have no doubt that He is!

Do you hear His words of comfort to you that says *"Come unto me all you who are weary and burdened, and I will give you rest* (Matt. 11:28, NIV)."

Today, I want to remind you that whatever your lot may be, you are not alone. God is with you! The storms of life come to us all, and when they do, we can anchor our hope in God, for He alone can steer us safely through life's stormy seas. "Why not cast your cares upon the Lord!"

Minister Debra Aiken

_____
_____
_____
_____
_____
_____
_____
_____
_____
_____
_____
_____
_____

THE PURPOSE FOR THE PAIN

"Beloved, think it not strange concerning the fiery trial, which is to try you, as though some strange thing happened unto you."
1 Peter 4:12

The Purpose for our Pain is the realization and understanding of the transition that takes place when God's handy work has been manifested through our faithfulness to His word. It is evidence of how strong the power of God is that brings us out of our darkest moments into His marvelous light. It demonstrates how God answers prayers and that His promises are true that He will never leave us, nor will He forsake us; that no weapon formed against us shall prosper; and that He really does know the plans for our lives.

He ordained us, sanctified us for His purpose, orders our very steps and leads us to our destined places of fulfillment for the Great Commission that He has commanded to all of His children. Our trials and tribulations come to make us strong, but the caveat is that it's not for us to keep to ourselves. God has purposed us to go into all of the world and spread the Good news of Jesus Christ; that He was born to be the Savior of the world; He lives so that we can live and become a new creature; He died to pay for and to save us from our sins, and He was resurrected that we may have eternal relationship with God.

The Purpose for the Pain is to allow God to birth new life in us over and over again so that we may be healed, delivered, set free and restored unto Him and a testimony to others that they may be saved.

Minister Sonja Pinckney Rhodes

IN THE WAITING

*"But they that wait upon the Lord shall renew their strength;
they shall mount up with wings as eagles; they shall run,
and not be weary; and they shall walk, and not faint."*
Isaiah 40:31

L ife's challenges can sap your energy. When a person loses their strength, they tend to disassociate themselves with others, make excuses to cancel appointments, stay home from church, and stay in bed. A loss of strength makes a person feel inadequate or unneeded. Feeling weak, unloved, or worthless results from a loss of hope. Isaiah shares a solution for such a depraved state. Wait on the LORD. Focus on the LORD to change one's perspective and fill one's thinking with biblical principles.

In the waiting process, a weary person faints in doing good. Once one loses interest in the people and work of the LORD, a reboot is vital. In the waiting process, one discovers their weak areas: flaws, sins, and misaligned perceptions. One may notice that their speech needs to be more seasoned with Godly words, some actions are wicked, or their thinking needs to be according to the teachings of Jesus Christ. The Lord God can renew your hope when one trusts in the Lord as the source of strength and courage. It only takes one verse or hymn to refresh one's mind. Focusing on God empowers one to shake off the fatigue and continue walking in His ways. Changing your perspective results in renewed strength to soar, run, and walk.

Dr. Pamela Gay

JESUS IS MY FRIEND

"A friend loves at all times, and a brother
is born for a time of adversity."
Proverbs 17:17

" **W** hat A Friend We Have in Jesus all our sins and grieves to bear. What a privilege to carry everything to God in prayer." This song is a great assurance in believing that we are never alone in this life and that we do not have to carry the heavy weights that life throws our way. God sent Jesus to be our Savior, Lord, and Friend. As our Friend, He is there to walk with us daily through the good and bad times. As our Friend, we can share our deepest emotions, sorrows, and pain with Him without a response of judgment. Yet, He is a good friend that holds us accountable in love. He is transparent with us like Jonathan was with David. We must be open to trusting Him and receiving His guidance. We can trust Him to lead us through those valleys of the shadow of death. We serve a God who loves us so much that He became human through Jesus Christ just to be present as our friend. Let us receive His love by showing our love as His friend.

Minister Dr. Nathalina Rogers-Tolbert

LASER FOCUS!

"Look straight ahead, and fix your eyes on what lies before you."
Proverbs 4:25

Stress often creeps in when we look back at past mistakes or look around, comparing ourselves to others. The result? Distraction, discouragement, and a loss of clarity. But the Word of God calls us to look ahead—to fix our eyes on the purpose He's placed before us. Think of light. A flashlight illuminates the path, helping us see in the dark. But a laser? A laser pierces, cuts, and burns. Both are light, but only one is focused enough to transform. This same principle applies to your spiritual journey. You cannot win the battles of life with the broad, unfocused glow of a flashlight when your purpose requires the precision and power of a laser. Your energy, time, and attention must be honed, not scattered. God has equipped you with everything you need to fulfill your purpose, but it requires focus. Stop looking back at regret or to the side at distractions. Instead, fix your eyes on the future God has for you. Sharpen your vision with prayer, discipline, and obedience. When you look within and focus like a laser, you'll cut through the noise, overcome obstacles, and step into the fullness of your calling. Today's Challenge: What distractions do you need to surrender to become laser-focused on your God-given purpose?

Reverend Randy Adkins Jr

BLESSED QUIETNESS

"And the work of righteousness will be peace, And the service
of righteousness, quietness and confidence forever."
Isaiah 32:17

D o you know the importance of finding moments of peace and quiet in this fast-paced world? It can be yours in God's quiet presence. You are called to pause, be still, and focus on the awareness of God's sovereignty on this glorious journey. I would like to recommend one of my favorite hymns to assist you along the way.

"Blessed Quietness." Listen to the words in this hymn. Joy is flowing like a river, since the comforter has come. He abides with us forever, makes the trusting heart His home. Blessed quietness, holy quietness, what assurance in my soul; on the stormy sea He speaks peace to me-how the billows cease to roll.

You can have God's Spiritual quietness with you when the billows cease to roll. He is available to you. Just allow His outpouring quietness to comfort you. His acts from above will change your condition on earth. Keep these two words in mind: Blessed is in the past tense, so you already have it. Quietness is absence of noise or bustle, with calmness in the Lord.

This life of faith in Christ Jesus, has a twofold blessing. Enjoy the peace and quietness of God's hand upon your life.

Minister Janet Williams-Johnson

Removing The Seed Of Satan From Our Lives

"When thou goest, thy steps shall not be straightened;
when thou runnest thou shalt not stumble."
Proverbs 4:12

Satan desires to sip us up like wheat. We must learn how to familiarize ourselves with His spiritual devices, by studying GOD'S word and praying in all things.

The Holy Spirit desires to lead us in every situation of our lives. This will happen if we allow HIM that spiritual permission so we will not lean on our understanding. Remember, Satan is a liar. He's a deceiver and He's the accuser of the brothers. Yes, remember, Eve was deceived by Satan. She was not paying attention to everything that God gave them to enjoy in the garden because Satan had her focus on the small tree **(Gen. 3:6-7).**

Again remember, Moses was not allowed to lead the people into the promised land because GOD told Him to speak to the rock, He got angry with the people and struck the rock **(Num. 20:8-11).** We see how the seed of anger kept Moses out of the Promised Land. What seeds of Satan are keeping you from completing your destiny of God? Let us not be Silent Christians, we have the power to bind Satan's Seeds of Adultery, Fornication, Uncleanness, Idolatry, Witchcraft, Hatred, and Strife. The list above is just a few of Satan's Evil Seeds!

Be BLESS and WALK in your AUTHORITY of the KINGDOM of GOD!

Evangelist Arthur Gaddist

WALK INTO YOUR SEASON OF VICTORY!

The next day the large crowd that had come to the feast heard that
Jesus was coming to Jerusalem. So they took branches of palm
trees and went out to meet Him, crying out, "Hosanna! Blessed is
He who comes in the name of the Lord, even the King of Israel!"
John 12:12-13

W hen I hear the word victory, terms such as success, winning, and triumph come to mind. But to truly achieve a goal, one must embrace the fact that struggles and challenges are not just obstacles, they're essential stepping stones on the path to success. Picture this: every great accomplishment in history was forged in the fires of adversity. Each challenge faced is an opportunity for growth, for learning, and for building resilience. When we encounter difficulties, it's a chance to dig deep, to push our limits, and to emerge stronger than before. Rather than shying away from these trials, let's lean into them. Remember the promises of God that are yes and amen and that you can do all things through Christ Jesus that strengthens you. Embracing the struggle not only makes the victory sweeter but also transforms us into better versions of ourselves. So, as you pursue your dreams, remember: every challenge you face is a vital part of your journey. Seize it, conquer it, and watch how it propels you toward your goals!

Minister Dr. Lucretia D. Wilson

WHO SIDE ARE YOU ON?

"For those who live according to the flesh set their minds
on the things of the flesh, but those who live according to
the Spirit, the things of the Spirit. For to be carnally minded
is death, but to be spiritually minded is life and peace."
Romans 8:5-6

As we navigate through life, we have a choice to either live in peace or in chaos. To live in peace is to be quickened by God through the Holy Spirit, and come under the authority of Jesus Christ. To live in death, or carnally minded, is to live under the world system, which are naturally minded and are not subject to the laws of God. The death that Paul is talking about is not a physical death, but a spiritual death. They only look at what they have attained in the natural, without God's help, success without being under the God head, God the Father, Jesus Christ, and the Holy Spirit. When they lose what they have achieved, some may lose their mind, some commit suicide. They have no greater power to call on but themselves. To live in true peace is to live under the authority of Jesus Christ the Lord. Who imparted in us the Holy Spirit.

Romans 14:17 *"For the kingdom of God is righteousness, and peace and joy in the Holy Spirit."* Ephesians 2:8 *"For by grace you have been saved through faith, and that not of yourselves; it is the gift of God."*

Reverend Graylan Richardson

CONVICTIONS VERSES ENVIRONMENT

"Do you have faith? Have it to yourself before God. Happy is
He who does not condemn himself in what He approves."
Romans 14:22

T hough the world around us may be in chaos, especially in this political season, we must hold on convictions, and not to influence by our environment. In this toxic time, we must draw even closer to God. We must stand by our convictions. The Holy Spirit, act as a compass to guide us through the difficulties and uncertainties in life (Proverbs 3:5-6). Hold fast to what you know to be true, even when faced with opposition. Stay true to yourself, and let your convictions, and the Holy Spirit will see you through.

Minister Rosalyn Brown

_____
_____
_____
_____
_____
_____
_____
_____
_____
_____
_____
_____
_____
_____
_____
_____
_____
_____
_____
_____
_____
_____
_____
_____
_____

The Gift of Favor – Called into Unknown Places

"God hath chosen the weak things of the world to
confound the things which are mighty."
I Corinthians 1:26-27

I want to begin by talking about Mary. There is something about Mary. The mother of Jesus of Nazareth. As we look closely at Mary, the Mother of Jesus' life, I believe it will allow us to look at our lives as God calls us into unknown places and spaces, but in the midst of uncertainty and unknowing and of being in the state of unqualified and unprepared of what is next, God wants you to know that He is with you. How can this be? God doesn't call the qualified; He qualifies the called.

Paul in I Corinthians 1:26-27 says it like this, brothers and sisters, think of what you were when you were called. Not many of you were wise by human standards, influential, not many were of noble birth, but God chose the foolish things of the world to shame the wise. God chose the weak things of the world to shame the strong. And the called is not intended for us to get the glory, because only God is worthy of all praise, glory and honor. It is by grace that you have been saved through faith. This is not from yourselves; it is the gift of God. Not by works so no one can boast. We can do all things through Christ who strengthens us. It lies in your perspective, your priorities and your source of power.

Minister Sonja Pinckney Rhodes

PAUSED FOR PURPOSE

"But those who wait on the LORD shall renew their
strength; They shall mount up with wings like eagles,
They shall run and not be weary, They shall walk and not faint."
Isaiah 40:31

Have you ever driven down a road and, suddenly the traffic slowed down to a stop? After a few minutes, things picked up, leaving you wondering what caused the delay. Frustration rises as you realize this pause has interrupted your plans. Being in a holding pattern is one of life's greatest challenges. It tests us, depending on what we are waiting for, how long it takes and why we are on hold. Impatience grows the longer it lasts.

Just as there are natural pauses, we sometimes experience a "spiritual" pause. Have you ever prayed for something and had to wait?

God already knew your needs and, formed a plan before you even asked.

Take heart; the waiting period is not a waste. God's timing may differ from yours but, He promises to answer in your time of need. Waiting on the Lord draws you closer to Him; is full of purpose and helps you evaluate your motives. It also teaches patience and resilience in faith.

Just think of how much you learn during the wait!

Reverend Valarie Pritchard

_____
_____
_____
_____
_____
_____
_____
_____
_____
_____
_____
_____
_____
_____
_____
_____

THE POWER OF LOVE

"And now these three remain: faith, hope and
love. But the greatest of these is love."
1 Corinthians 13:13

L ove is the essence of God's character and the foundation of our faith. It is a love that is patient, kind, and unfailing. When we embody God's love, we reflect His heart to those around us. Take time today to love sacrificially, even when it's difficult. Let God's love flow through you.

Reflection Question: How can you demonstrate God's love to someone today, and where might God wish for His love to be shared?

Reverend Dr. Byron L. Benton
Senior Pastor

JULY

"Be strong and take heart,
all you who hope in the Lord."

Psalm 31:24

SHARING YOUR GIFTS TO EDIFY OTHERS

"Each of you should use whatever gift you have
received to serve others, as faithful
stewards of God's grace in its various forms."
1 Peter 4:10

Your gifts are not for your glory, but for God's purposes. By sharing your talents, time, and resources, you strengthen the body of Christ. Consider how you can use your unique gifts to serve others and glorify God.

Reflection Question: How might you use your God-given gifts to bless someone today?

Reverend Dr. Byron L. Benton
Senior Pastor

Trust In God + Hope = Strong Foundation

"For in this hope, we were saved. But hope that is seen is no hope at all. Who hopes for what they already have?"
Romans 8:24

As we experience the highs and lows of life, we can feel a range of emotions, from being on top of the world to being tossed about beyond our control. What do you do amid an ever-changing life, an ever-changing world? Applying these steps to every situation will keep you in the safety of the almighty.

1. Acknowledge God-we must believe that He Is! He's the Alpha and Omega, the beginning and end of all things that are and are to come. His omnipotence (unlimited power), omnipresence (everywhere), and sovereignty rule and reign forever.
2. Trust—Proverbs 3:5 says, (ESV) Trust in the LCRD with all your heart, and do not lean on your own understanding. In all your ways, acknowledge Him, and He will make straight your paths.
3. Hear and obey His word. Cultivate your ear, heart, and spirit to recognize the voice and presence of God. Pray that He gives you ears to hear what He says in the spirit. Don't move before or after His direction, but obediently respond and move with Him.
4. Keep clean hands and a pure heart before God. Because we all sin and fall short of the glory of God, we can only reach our mediator, Jesus Christ, who intercedes for us. Jesus is the cornerstone of our strong foundation. That security keeps us anchored through every celebration and storm.

Minister Anna M. Montgomery

_____
_____
_____
_____
_____
_____
_____
_____
_____
_____
_____

FORGIVENESS

"Get rid of all bitterness, rage and anger, brawling and slander,
along with every form of malice. Be kind and compassionate to one
another, forgiving each other, just as in Christ God forgave you."
Ephesians 4:31-32

Forgiveness! What? You are asking me to forgive someone who has emotionally and psychologically abused me for years? Are you really asking me to forgive the person who violated me over and over again? You are joking, right? No, absolutely not! God commands it!

I want to make sure I am hearing what you are saying, because forgiving my abuser makes no sense to me, after all the hurt and pain I endured from that person for so many years. Without a doubt, you are hearing me correctly. God commands us to "Put aside all bitterness, losing our temper, anger, shouting, and slander, along with every other evil (Eph 2:31, CEB)".

We are commanded to remove ourselves from such behaviors. Instead, God is calling us to be a people who are kind one to another, tenderhearted, and forgiving of each other, even as He forgave us in Christ (Eph. 2:32 ESV)".

As Christians, when we learn to let go of these negative emotions that God is calling us to rid ourselves of, not only will we be able to freely walk in newness of life, move forward in our relationship with God and others, but we will also be able to live an impactful life of experiencing God's presence and His power in a much greater way as we minister the Gospel of Jesus Christ to others.

Let's walk together in the love language called "forgiveness," so that we may be witnesses for Christ. God Commands it!

Minister Debra Aiken

STEP INTO THE LIGHT

"Thy word is a lamp unto my feet, and a light unto my path."
Psalm 119:105

As long as you live by the word of God, you never have to be in the dark again.

You never have to remain confused about which path to take. You never have to go through life alone, struggling to find your way. It is exciting to know that the word of God will give you all the light you need every day of your life if you will allow it to! Build your faith in His Word and renew your commitment to it as you make this confession today:

"Father, in the Name of Jesus, I commit myself to walk in Your Word. I recognize that Your Word is steadfast, eternal, and I trust my life to its provisions. You have sent Your Word into my heart. I meditate on it day and night so that I may act on it. Your Word is abiding in my spirit, and it is growing mightily in me.

"I recognize the strategies and deceits of the enemy." I am confident, Father, that you are at work in me both to will and to do Your good pleasure. I exalt Your Word. I hold it in high esteem and give it first place in my life. I boldly and confidently say that my heart is fixed and established on a solid foundation. The Living word of God!

Minister Carmen S. Bowman

THE JOY OF THE LORD

"The joy of the Lord is our strength."
Nehemiah 8:10

T he joy of the Lord is not just a fleeting emotion or a reaction to circumstances; it is a deep, abiding peace that transcends the highs and lows of life. It is the strength that comes from knowing God is with us, that His love never fails, and that His promises are sure. In the midst of trials, when we feel weary or discouraged, the joy of the Lord is a reminder that we are never alone.

This joy is not dependent on what we have or don't have, but on who He is. It is the inner confidence that God is good, that He is faithful, and that He is working all things together for our good. When we choose to rejoice in His presence, despite our circumstances, we tap into a wellspring of strength that refreshes our souls and enables us to keep moving forward.

Joy in the Lord is also contagious. It is a light that shines brightly in a dark world, drawing others to experience the same peace and hope we have found in Him. As we delight in God's goodness, our hearts become more attuned to His presence, and we discover a joy that is unshakeable, no matter what life may bring.

Remember, joy in the Lord is not a goal to be achieved but a gift to be received. Let it overflow in your heart today, and let it carry you through every moment with grace and hope. The joy of the Lord is truly our strength.

Minister Sonja Pinckney Rhodes

LIVING IN HOPE

"The Lord delights in those who fear Him, who
put their hope in His unfailing love."
Psalm 147:11

G od delights in our hope. Celebrate hope on the days it comes easily. Ask our Lord Jesus to supply you with an extra dose of hope on the days it comes harder. Don't give up! Hold to God's Unchanging hand!!!

Reverend Gloria Lightfoot

No Barriers: Christ Closed The Gap

*When Jesus was crucified, the earth trembled, rocks split — and
something remarkable happened in the temple: "At that moment
the curtain of the temple was torn in two from top to bottom."*
Matthew 27:51

That curtain wasn't just a piece of fabric — it represented the ultimate barrier, the separation between God and humanity. Only a select few could stand in His presence, and only under strict conditions. But at the moment of Christ's death, that barrier was destroyed. Jesus closed the gap and opened the way for all people, regardless of status, background, or ability, to have full access to God.

Today, we still see gaps — especially in education, where despite many efforts, some students remain cut off from the resources and opportunities they need to grow and flourish. The achievement gap is a painful reminder of the brokenness in human systems.

But the Good News reminds us: in Christ, there are no barriers. His sacrifice tore down the greatest wall of separation. While we continue to work for fairness and access here on earth, we can rejoice knowing the door to God's presence is already wide open. No limitations. No qualifications. Just grace. So let us live, teach, and serve with joy — trusting in the One who breaks down every barrier.

Dear Lord, thank You for tearing down the barriers that kept us from Your presence. While we see gaps and divides all around us, remind us that You have already made a way for all. Strengthen us to reflect Your love by helping lift others, and fill us with joy as we walk in Your freedom. In Jesus' name, Amen.

Minister Rhulaunda Donald

Not Crushed, Not Forsaken

"We are hard-pressed on every side, but not crushed;
perplexed, but not in despair; persecuted, but not
abandoned; struck down, but not destroyed."
2 Corinthians 4:8–9

Y ou may feel surrounded by pressure, your plans unraveling in your hands. But take heart—you are not crushed. Life's trials can bring you to your knees, but they cannot undo the promises of God. Paul's words remind us that being perplexed isn't the same as being lost. Feeling struck down doesn't mean you're finished. When everything feels uncertain, God remains constant. He walks with you through the fire, not around it. He strengthens your resolve, not just your results. And when you're at your lowest, God doesn't look away—He draws nearer. Even in your deepest disappointment, you are not abandoned. God is still writing your story, even in the pauses. Your weariness may be real, but so is your resilience. Remember: God hasn't just preserved you —He's preparing you.

Dr. Da'rrell Ravenell

JESUS, JUSTICE, COMFORT AND ETERNITY

"Therefore, comfort each other and edify one
another, just as you also are doing."
Thessalonians 5:11

The "C" in Justice stands for comfort. God can comfort us and make His presence known in all situations. He is with us in the good times and the bad times. He comforts us as we grieve the transition of a loved one. He comforts us when a relationship sours. He comforts us in all our losses if we would only turn to Him. He comforts the families whose loved ones died due to gun violence or because of the unjust policies and procedures in our Justice System, where their loved one has to go to jail.

The "E" in Justice stands for eternity. This should be the goal of all God's people. We must decide where we will spend eternity. Shall it be in the everlasting fire or shall it be with Jesus, the Lamb who gave His life for us so that we can be with Him forever and ever. *"He has made everything beautiful in its time. Also, He has put eternity in their hearts, except that no one can find out the work that God does from beginning to end* (Ecclesiastes 3:11)."

Reverend Brenda Stallings

THE WORK OF AN EVANGELIST

"But you, keep your head in all situations, endure hardship, do the work of an evangelist, discharge all the duties of your ministry."
Timothy 4:5

E veryone should have someone to mentor or a mentee to guide in the things of God. Paul gives Timothy sound advice about fulfilling His duties in ministry. Do not lose your temper or be a hothead. People can be intimidated by those who yell or fail to listen to the whole story. A person who loses His temper can be a discouragement or turn-off to others. To lose your temper or become easily aggravated is a sign of Christian immaturity.

The work of an evangelist is to endure people so that the training environment is conducive for learning. Fear and intimidation are forms of bullying. Good leaders demonstrate mercy and grace, so the followers are discipled using Jesus' model of love and compassion. One must have a teachable spirit. Doing the work of an evangelist means developing your crafts and skillfully doing what God directs. Share the word of God without judging others. Be patient yet alert to the needs of those in your sphere of influence. Live the message you speak, sing, or teach to others. As the days pass, all must do the work of an evangelist to share God's plan of salvation with the world. Do not be impatient. Perform your evangelistic duties with love.

Dr. Pamela Gay

God's Favor

"For by grace are ye saved through faith; and
that not of yourselves: it is the gift of God."
Ephesians 2:8

Favor is when God smiles upon you and delights in your life. It's His special grace that makes a way when there seems to be no way. Favor opens doors that no man can shut and closes doors that no man can open. It keeps you from falling and provides what no one else can. Favor is the supernatural intervention of God that brings blessings and breakthroughs beyond human understanding.

Proverbs 20:21 reminds us that while some will choose great riches, silver, and gold, the true blessing lies in God's favor. Favor is a gift that cannot be earned or bought—it is freely given by God to those who trust in Him. When you walk in favor, it means that God is with you, He's got you, and His hand is upon your life.

Favor means that no weapon formed against you will prosper, no matter the circumstances. It means that, even when others oppose you, God is for you. His favor protects, provides, and positions you for success in ways that human effort cannot achieve.

Above all, favor brings supernatural increase, victory, and eternal life. Through God's grace, we have been saved, and His favor secures our future. When you walk in favor, you are walking in the abundant life He has promised, a life full of purpose, peace, and power. So, choose favor—because with God's favor, all things are possible.

Minister Sonja Pinckney Rhodes

MY HOPE

"Now the God of hope fill you with all joy and peace in believing,
that ye may abound in hope, through the power of the Holy Ghost."
Romans 15: 13

H ope is a powerful force, something that anchors the soul even in the stormiest seasons of life. Hope is a confident expectation that something good is coming, even when everything around me suggests otherwise. In difficult times such as what we have faced in our country concerning the elections, it's easy to lose sight of hope. When things don't go as planned , or when life feels overwhelmed. The scripture tells us that as Believers we can trust God's promises, and His faithfulness. I believe that God works all things for our good, even when we can't see the bigger picture. I love singing the song, "My hope is built on nothing less Than Jesus' blood and righteousness, I dare not trust the sweetest frame But wholly lean on Jesus' name." Hope gives me the strength to keep moving forward. Hope encourages me when I'm exhausted, and it encourages me to look beyond my present difficulties to the possibilities ahead. Hope doesn't mean everything will be easy, but it does mean that no matter what, I'm never alone. I know that in the midst of uncertainty, I can hold on to the hope that better days are ahead, and that God is with me every step of the way. Today, I choose Hope and I'm trusting that things will get better.

Reverend Julette M. Scott

OBTAINING PERFECT PEACE

"So, Gideon built an altar to the Lord there and called it The Lord
Is Peace. To this day it stands in Ophrah of the Abiezrites."
Judges 6:24

I n my senior year of high school, I was given an English assignment that required me to write a narrative based on the poem written by Henry Wadsworth Longfellow *"Lines Written a Few Miles above Tintern Abbey."* The assignment required me to find a place that was like the setting in the poem that brought me peace. From this assignment I soon found out that everyone's version of peace was different. I wrote about how I found peace in a person and not a place, only to find out later on that this person would soon reject me. I learned from this experience that the peace that comes with places, people, and things, is always temporary because they pass away and when they pass away the peace that they brought passes away also. But God is our eternal Peace that never leaves us. When we make God our peace, this allows us to take perfect, eternal peace with us wherever we go. Gideon built an altar and called it "The Lord is Peace," although this altar was stationary it was a symbol of Gods unchanging constant Peace. When we search for peace, let us first look to the perfect Peace of the Lord.

Minister Tristan Simmons

Unshakable Faith

"Therefore, my beloved brethren, be ye steadfast, immovable, always abounding in the work of the Lord, forasmuch as ye know that your labor is not in vain in the Lord."
1 Corinthians 15:58

Many times, situations occur in life that can cause doubt and question whether we heard the voice of God through His Holy Spirit about His instructions for life. Those distractors can even manifest uncertainties about our relationship with God. A relationship that has stood the test of time, hurricanes, and storms greater than blizzards, hail, wind, and bomb cyclones. A relationship that is built upon the rock and not sinking sand. Supernatural rock. Remember, Saints, our blessed assurance is to remain fixed on what was, is, and is to come through our Lord and Savior, Jesus Christ. Jesus is the same yesterday, today, and forever. We must look to the hills from whence cometh our help, knowing that our help cometh from the Lord our God who made heaven and earth. The writer in 1 Corinthians puts it this way, *"Be ye steadfast, immovable, always excelling and doing your best and more than is needed, being perpetually aware that your labor, even to the point of exhaustion, in the Lord is not futile nor wasted and that it is never without purpose."*

Minister Dr. Lucretia D. Wilson

Justice, Without Jesus There Is No Justice

"He has made everything beautiful in its time. He has also set eternity in the human heart; yet no one can fathom what God has done from beginning to end."
Ecclesiastes 3:11

T he "E" in Justice stands for eternity. This should be the goal of all God's people. We must decide where we will spend eternity. Shall it be in the everlasting fire of shall it be with Jesus, the Lamb who gave His life for us so that we can be with Him forever and ever.

Ecclesiastes 3:11 *"He has made everything beautiful in its time. Also, He has put eternity in their hearts, except that no one can find out the work that God does from beginning to end."*

Without Jesus, there is no justice. Jesus is in front of us, standing together in unity, to bring salvation to the lost in order to increase the Kingdom of God. Trusting in the Lord is to know things will get better, knowing that inspiration is necessary in order to keep the people engaged and putting the word in their hearts.

When we have compassion for the masses and bring them comfort in all situations, the heart of the people will belong to our Savior, Jesus Christ. Taking and sharing the fruits of the Spirit will allow us as disciples of Christ to show justice in all we do and reach our destination in eternity where we will be able to rest from our labors and sit and have a little talk with Jesus and tell Him how we made it over.

Reverend Dr. Brenda Joyce Stallings

THE INVITATION

"Come to me, all you who are weary and
burdened, and I will give you rest."
Matthew 11:28

This message is for all those who are tired, weary, worn out and burned out.

In this passage of Scripture the Lord is sending out an invitation. I'm sure everyone has received an invitation at one time or another. A birthday party, a wedding, a graduation, or a baby's dedication. In Matthew 11:28 the first word in Jesus's invitation is, "Come." Jesus wants you to come to Him.

Since we can't physically come to Jesus because Jesus is in heaven, we come to Jesus by believing in Him, trusting Him and obeying His word. I like the fact that *Jesus invites all*. He does not have any special specifications as far as race, color, rich or poor, male or female. It is an open invitation for all. The tired, the weary, those who are physically, mentally or emotionally drained.

Some are carrying the burdens of humanity, as well as their own burdens. They are exhausted. It is too much to bear. Hook up with Jesus! Jesus offers us rest. His rest. There you will find peace of mind. He is kind, gentle and He will carry your burdens for you. With Jesus, you will find peace of mind and rest for the soul. When you come to Jesus, His truth will greet you at the door of your heart. What a wonderful invitation.

Reverend Brenda Smalls-Robinson

No Condemnation in Christ

"Therefore, there is now no condemnation
for those who are in Christ Jesus."
Romans 8:1

Sometimes, it's easy to feel like we're not good enough — especially when we make mistakes or fall short of what we think we should be. In school, at home, or in our relationships, it can feel like we're constantly being judged or criticized. But there's incredible freedom in knowing that, in Christ, there is no condemnation.

Romans 8:1 says, *"Therefore, there is now no condemnation for those who are in Christ Jesus."* This means that when we accept Jesus into our lives, we are no longer defined by our failures or mistakes. God doesn't hold our past sins against us, and He doesn't condemn us for the things we've done wrong. Instead, He offers forgiveness, grace, and a fresh start.

For example, when Jake failed His math test, He felt embarrassed and discouraged. He thought, "I've messed up. I'm not good enough." But then He remembered what He had learned in church — that in Christ, He was not defined by His failures. He prayed and asked God for strength to do better next time. Instead of letting condemnation drag Him down, Jake found hope in God's grace.

When we accept God's love and forgiveness, we don't need to carry the weight of guilt. In Christ, we are made new, and we can move forward with confidence, knowing that we are free from condemnation and loved unconditionally.

Minister Sonja Pinckney Rhodes

_____
_____
_____
_____
_____
_____
_____
_____
_____
_____
_____
_____
_____

WHY AM I NOT HEALED? YOU MUST ASK GOD.

"O Lord my God, I cried unto thee, and thou hast healed me."
Psalms 30:2

The question was asked, Why am I not healed? I must declare to you that with the HOLY SPIRIT'S permission, you were already healed when Jesus hung on the cross. His blood cleanses our sickness, diseases, and hurt sins. I must remind you that there are no sicknesses or diseases in Heaven. If this is so, which do I believe?

In the book, **Matthew 9:10** states Thy Kingdom Come, thy will be done on Earth as it is in Heaven. If this is so, which I do believe, we must learn in the spirit to speak life, NOT death. **Proverbs 13:21**

Let's keep believing, keep standing, and keep declaring our Faith in every situation and/or circumstances that come up against us. We must trust the power of PRAYER to move mountains in our lives. The woman with the issue of blood believed her FAITH could move mountains. **Matt. 9:19-20**

I believe that our GOD heals in many ways.

Matt. 9:23-24 - Jesus touched the ruler's daughter, and she came back to life.

In Luke 13:11, there was a woman who had a spirit of infirmity for eighteen long years. She was unable to lift herself up. When JESUS saw her, He called her to Him and spoke, and instantly the woman was loosed from her infirmities. He spoke Life, not Death, and she was healed.

Evangelist Arthur Gaddist

_____
_____
_____
_____
_____
_____
_____
_____
_____
_____
_____
_____
_____
_____

AUGUST

"See, I am doing a new thing! Now it springs up; do you not perceive it? I am making a way in the wilderness and streams in the wasteland."

Isaiah 43:19 (NIV)

THE POWER OF LOVE

"And now these three remain: faith, hope and
love. But the greatest of these is love."
1 Corinthians 13:13

L ove is the essence of God's character and the foundation of our faith. It is a love that is patient, kind, and unfailing. When we embody God's love, we reflect His heart to those around us. Take time today to love sacrificially, even when it's difficult. Let God's love flow through you.

Reflection Question: How can you demonstrate God's love to someone today, and where might God wish for His love to be shared?

Reverend Dr. Byron L. Benton
Senior Pastor

_____
_____
_____
_____
_____
_____
_____
_____
_____
_____
_____
_____
_____
_____
_____
_____
_____
_____
_____
_____
_____
_____
_____
_____

HOPE FOR RESTORATION

"Then Joseph said to His brothers, 'Come close to me.'...
'I am your brother Joseph, the one you sold into Egypt! And
now, do not be distressed or angry with yourselves... because
it was to save lives that God sent me ahead of you."
Genesis 45:4–5

Broken friendships can leave lasting wounds. Betrayal, misunderstanding, or distance can build walls that seem too high to ever climb again. Yet the story of Joseph gives us hope. Joseph had every right to be bitter. His brothers had stripped Him of His coat, His freedom, and nearly His life. But when the moment of reckoning came, Joseph didn't retaliate — He reached out. Through tears and trembling words, He invited His brothers close and offered forgiveness instead of revenge.

What changed the outcome? Joseph saw God's hand in the pain. He understood that what others meant for harm, God used for good. That perspective allowed His heart to heal — and made room for reconciliation.

If God can restore a relationship that broken, imagine what He can do with ours.

Maybe you're carrying the weight of a fractured friendship. Maybe you've given up hope that it could ever be whole again. But the God who brought Joseph and His brothers back together still heals hearts today. Restoration is possible — not because we're strong, but because *He* is.

Take the first step. Forgive. Reach out. Believe again.

God still writes redemption stories.

Dear Lord, thank You for being a God who restores. Heal the broken places in our hearts and give us the courage to forgive as You forgive. Where friendships have fallen apart, breathe new life. Teach us to trust Your timing and see Your hand in every story — even the painful ones. In Jesus' name, Amen.

Minister Rhulaunda Donald

GOD STILL DELIVERS

"Many are the afflictions of the righteous: but
the Lord delivereth Him out of them all."
Psalm 34:19

T rouble doesn't mean you're forsaken. In fact, Scripture tells us that the righteous will face many afflictions. But affliction is not the end of the story — deliverance is. God is not absent in the fire; He steps into it with you. He does not abandon you in the lion's den; He shuts the mouths of what should have devoured you. He is a deliverer — not just in theory, but in your reality.

Every time you felt like giving up and didn't — that was deliverance. Every time you cried out in desperation and found strength to take one more step — that was deliverance. Sometimes we wait for dramatic miracles, and miss the quiet ones that carry us through our days.

This promise in Psalm 34 is both comfort and call. Comfort, because God sees your suffering and will bring you out. Call, because deliverance is not just escape — it's transformation. You won't leave the fire the same person who entered it.

So stand firm. Keep praying. Keep hoping. Keep trusting that God still delivers. Not just once, but every time you need Him. Out of all of them.

Minister Sonja Pinckney Rhodes

Unplanned Detours

*"For I know the plans I have for you," says the
Lord. "They are plans for good and not for
disaster, to give you a future and a hope."*
Jeremiah 29:11

As we travel, we constantly see construction—older roads, highways, and bridges being torn down while new ones are being built. People who have taken these familiar routes for years are now finding themselves needing to find alternate paths.

What happens when God changes the course of your life, forcing you to take a detour? There are spiritual bridges in our lives that God intentionally dismantles to prevent us from continuing down paths that don't lead where we need to go. If these bridges are not removed, we might keep crossing them indefinitely. Some paths lead nowhere, while others feel so comfortable that we begin to set our own course, ignoring the stop, danger, and yield signs God has placed along the way.

God knows that if we keep going down certain roads, we may never reach the destination He has planned for us. So, thank God for every detour. He is the ultimate guide and will lead you safely along life's path.

Reverend Valarie Pritchard

THE POWER OF TRANSFORMATION

"And do not be conformed to this world, but be transformed by
the renewing of your mind, that by testing you may discern what
is the will of God, what is good and acceptable and perfect."
Romans 12:2

This scripture resonates in three important factors for believers in Christ, in having a transformed mind: Humility, Seeking, and Turning.

Humility: Recognizing our limitations and acknowledging our need for growth is the first step towards positive change. It allows us to be open to learning and receiving guidance.

Seeking: Actively pursuing a connection, whether it's with God, a mentor, or a community, demonstrates a commitment to personal development. It's about reaching out and seeking support, wisdom, and inspiration.

Turning: Making a conscious decision to turn away from harmful paths requires courage and determination. It's about letting go of negative habits, toxic relationships, and self-destructive behaviors.

When we combine these three elements, we unlock the potential for profound transformation. We open ourselves up to hope, renewal, and a brighter future.

This message is a powerful reminder that change is possible, and it's within our reach. By embracing humility, seeking connection, and turning towards a better path, we can experience the extraordinary.

Minister Rosalyn Brown

JOY VS. HAPPINESS

*"Then He said unto them, Go your way, eat the fat, and drink
the sweet, and send portions unto them for whom nothing
is prepared: for this day is holy unto our Lord: neither be
ye sorry; for the joy of the LORD is your strength."*
Nehemiah 8:10

W e have all heard the song, so don't worry; be happy. The song reminds us, *"That which hath been is that which shall be, and that which hath been done is that which shall be done: and there is no new thing under the sun* (Ecclesiastes 1:9 ASV)." Let me explain. A professor used the words to the song to help alleviate stress and anxiety related to the outcomes of a difficult exam. During an assignment years ago, a Pastor asked, "What is the difference between happiness and joy?" As I prayed for the response, I asked a question. He immediately responded that happiness is temporary, and joy is eternal. Beloved, why walk in a temporary fix when you can have the everlasting joy of the Lord? Scripture states that the joy of the Lord is your strength. Believe it! The strength of the Lord is your joy. Joy is not just a feeling; it's a transformative force. This transformative power of joy gives us hope and inspires us to bring about positive change in our lives. As one of the nine fruits of the Holy Spirit, joy can change us. Strength, too, is an attribute of the Father. So, beloved, desire the greater. Let's allow the eternal joy of the Lord to penetrate our hearts and transform us. As we transition through these seasons of hope, being inspired by the profound power of joy to bring about positive changes in our lives, identify practical ways to cultivate joy daily.

Minister Dr. Lucretia D. Wilson

ALREADY DONE, BUT NOT YET FULFILLED

Then He closed the book and gave it back to the attendant
and sat down. And the eyes of all who were in the
synagogue were fixed on Him. And He began to say to
them, "Today this Scripture is fulfilled in your hearing."
Luke 4:20-21

J esus entered the synagogue on that sabbath day and read these words, *"The Spirit of the Lord is upon Me, because He has anointed me to preach the gospel to the poor; He has sent me to heal the brokenhearted, to proclaim liberty to the captives and recovery of sight to the blind, to set at liberty those who are oppressed; to proclaim the acceptable year of the Lord (Isa. 61:1-2)."*

Jesus only read a portion of Isaiah to proclaim that He was the Messiah they had been waiting for. The people wanted immediate justice, revenge and judgement against their enemies. However, we are all guilty of sin and under the Judgment of God.

Therefore, Jesus had to first secure our way for salvation on the cross. At Jesus' second coming He will fulfill the prophecy of Isaiah 61 in its entirety in verses 3-11. In Jesus Christ, the victory has already been won and there is a day when everything will be fulfilled on earth. Jesus is going to finish what He started.

Reverend Leonard Bailey

THE FRINGE

"And these are but the outer fringe of His works;
how faint the whisper we hear of Him! Who then
can understand the thunder of His power?"
Job 26:14

The incomprehensibility of our God has people, for centuries, seeking to figure Him out. God's love towards people who may seem unlovable is incomprehensible. The Lord God's supremacy in answering to no-one is mind-blowing. The outer fringe of God's works is a small piece of the power of God. Never mistake God as merely a larger form of humanity. God is the Creator of humanity. Complete comprehension of God's splendor is yet to be revealed to humanity. God is the infinite (endless, unlimited) deity.

Humanity possesses a finite (limited) mind that cannot fully comprehend the totality of God Almighty. The edge or border of knowledge that humanity receives is still not enough to convince all of humanity to serve God without reservations. God will never overload the minds of humanity. Our God progressively reveals Himself to humanity so everyone can come to know Him for themselves. God meets you where you are and reveals himself in stages. Our God whispers to us instead of yelling. No one can comprehend the fullness of God, especially since we cannot comprehend the fringe. God, in His tender mercy, reveals just enough of himself to draw us to Him gently. God sent His Son to help humanity know Him. Study the Scriptures to learn a fringe of the Incomprehensive God.

Dr. Pamela Gay

THE WAY OUT

*"The temptations in your life are no different from what
others experience. And God is faithful. He will not allow the
temptation to be more than you can stand. When you are
tempted, He will show you a way out so that you can endure."*
1 Corinthians 10:13

Temptation is universal. It's not a sign of weakness or failure—it's part of the human experience. The good news? You're not the only one facing it, and you're not alone in the fight. God never promises a temptation-free life, but He does promise this: you will never face more than you can endure. With every temptation, there's a way out—a lifeline provided by a faithful God who is invested in your victory. When the pressure feels overwhelming, remember that God's strength is greater than your weakness. Look for the escape He's provided. It might be a whispered prayer, a verse that comes to mind, or the courage to step away from the situation. Whatever it is, take it. Victory over temptation isn't about perfection—it's about perseverance. Each time you choose God's way, you become stronger, more equipped to walk in righteousness. You're not just enduring; you're becoming the mighty, righteous warrior He's called you to be. Today's Prayer: Lord, thank You for Your faithfulness. Lead me to victory as I overcome the battles of temptation. Strengthen me to endure, and open my eyes to see the way out You've prepared. Today's Challenge: Identify one area where you face temptation. Pray for God's strength and watch for His escape route. Choose victory today!

Reverend Randy Adkins Jr.

God Wants To Work In You

*"Therefore, my dear friends, as you have always obeyed—not only
in my presence, but now much more in my absence—continue to
work out your salvation with fear and trembling, for it is God who
works in you to will and to act in order to fulfill His good purpose."*
Philippians 2:12 – 13

For God to do this work in us, we must be committed. We must be committed to and dependent on God. It is not a dependence on what we can do for ourselves but a reliance on God. We must rely on and trust that God works in and on us. Whether things are going well or not, we must always trust that God is working for His good purpose. We must be willing to be used by God whenever and however He desires. Not when we want Him to move or how we want Him to move but trusting and depending on Him. He knows what is best for us. Am I talking to you? It is so easy to rely on yourself...especially when you are accustomed to doing things without the help of others. But we have to be willing to feel and be uncomfortable. Being uncomfortable suggests that you are allowing God to work on you. God wants us to give attention to His work in us. When we allow Him to work in us, we experience transformation...transformation of our minds and our hearts. When He works on us, we experience spiritual growth and our behaviors change. All of this is for His good purpose. Will you let Him work in you?

Reverend L. Michelle Mitchell

YES, JESUS STILL LOVES ME

Jesus answered, "I tell you, not seven
times, but seventy-seven times."
Matthew 18:21-22

Jesus Loves Me was a song that most of us heard and sang when we were young. It was an affirmation song that if we felt that no one loved us, we knew that Jesus did. It went something like this Yes, Jesus loves me! Yes, Jesus loves me! Yes, Jesus loves me! The Bible tells me so." And we felt that if the Bible said it, it must be true. Jesus loves me. Jesus loves me despite me. Jesus is love. What an awesome love story about how someone loves us so much that He died for our sins. And no matter the backstories of life, He still loves us. Not only that even when we commit acts of sin knowingly and unknowingly, He STILL loves us. God forgives us daily so, should we? And the answer remains, yes, at least seventy times seven. Let the Holy Spirit lead you.

Minister Dr. Nathalina Rogers-Tolbert

REJOICE

"Always be full of joy in the Lord; I say it again, rejoice!"
Philippians 4:4

C onsider for a minute the word "rejoice." It is identified as a verb that one may feel or show great joy of delight with spontaneity or directness. Biblically, "rejoice" is "charior" a Greek word meaning to be favorably disposed to God's grace. Sounds great, does it? Yet, there are circumstances, disappointments, conflicts, and unhealthy situations that pop-up in your life during this spiritual journey.

I pondered this verse during a devotional moment as I am sure you may have a time or two. As a child of God, you are called to joy, not to hopelessness and shame. You are called to "faith" the substance of things hoped for, and the evidence of things not seen.

Know this my brothers and sisters, this word "rejoice" is so important to your spiritual walk, that Apostle Paul used the word 9 times in one letter and Luke used it 11 times in the gospel. So, what are you waiting to do?

Every day that the Lord grants you, your family, and friends is a day to rejoice!

Minister Janet Williams-Johnson

LORD, WHY THE PAIN?

"Blessed are those who are persecuted for righteousness'
sake, For theirs is the kingdom of heaven."
St. Matthew 5:10

I n the summer of 2007, I found myself questioning the overwhelming presence of pain and suffering in my life. As I knelt in prayer, I asked, "Lord, why all this pain?" In that moment, I felt the gentle yet powerful words of Jesus echo from the pages of Scripture specifically 1 Peter 4:12-14 and Romans 8:17. These verses reminded me that God's Spirit and glory rest on those who endure trials. Rather than being surprised by suffering, I embraced it as an integral part of my faith journey. I learned to rejoice in the sufferings of Christ, understanding that such trials bring me closer to Him. When I face adversity for His sake, I am blessed for the Spirit of glory that resides within me. Jesus spoke about persecution as a purifying tool, one that cleanses our hearts and refines our lives. It is through this process of suffering that we are equipped for greater service and made stronger in our faith. The journey isn't easy, and it is common to feel overwhelmed, but realize the importance of not beating yourself up during these moments. Instead, lean into the safety of Jesus' arms, finding solace and strength. The trials may bring tears but hold onto the promise that *"Weeping may endure for a night, but joy comes in the morning."* In this assurance, proclaim with confidence that, it's morning time, and a new season of joy awaits, filled with hope and purpose.

Minister Dr. Lucretia D. Wilson

_____
_____
_____
_____
_____
_____
_____
_____
_____
_____
_____
_____
_____
_____

THE ALL-SUFFICIENT GOD: OUR PROVIDER AND STRENGTH

"The Lord will provide."
Genesis 22:14

The concept of God as "all-sufficient" speaks to His limitless nature and His ability to meet every need, both spiritually and materially. In Scripture, God reveals Himself as Jehovah-Jireh, meaning *"The Lord will provide"* (Genesis 22:14). This title emphasizes God's unchanging provision for His people, demonstrating that He is more than capable of supplying everything we need — whether for daily sustenance, emotional strength, or spiritual nourishment.

God's sufficiency is evident throughout the Bible. In Psalm 23:1, David declares, "The Lord is my shepherd; I shall not want," affirming that in God's presence, we lack nothing. He is not just a provider but the source of all we need — our peace, joy, wisdom, and security. Through Jesus Christ, God has given us the ultimate provision: salvation and eternal life, available by grace alone.

The all-sufficiency of God extends to all areas of our lives. When we face trials, God's strength is sufficient to sustain us (2 Corinthians 12:9). When we feel weak, He is our refuge and support. His grace is sufficient to cover our shortcomings, and His wisdom is more than enough to guide us through any circumstance.

Ultimately, the all-sufficient God calls us to trust Him completely, knowing that He will never fail to meet our needs according to His perfect will. In Him, we find everything we need to thrive in faith and life.

Minister Sonja Pinckney Rhodes

CALL JESUS

"The book of Revelation can be intimidating for
many believers, but let me break down what's
In John's vision, He is in the throne room of God. The throne
room features angels, 24 elders who likely represent the
12 tribes of Israel and the 12 disciples of Jesus, and other
beings. There's a throne at the center that the elders and
John struggle to even look at because it's so bright."
Revelation 5:1-14

There's a scroll that likely represents God's plans but it's sealed, and there is no one worthy to open the scroll. John begins to weep because of this. And once everyone is in despair, that's when a slain lamb appears. The lamb, who represents Jesus, is sitting on the throne, and He is declared worthy to open the scroll.

The text shows us; Jesus is not just a nice guy. Jesus Christ is God.

All power has been given to Him on Heaven and on Earth.

Take note of when Jesus appears in the text. When we are heartbroken and sad, Jesus appears. When we're about to give up hope, Jesus appears. When there's a task that no one else can do or a problem no one else can fix, that's when Jesus appears.

If there are things in your life that no one seems to be able to fix, call Jesus. If you're sinking into depression, call Jesus. And if the only one who can fix your problem is God, call Jesus.

Minister Kon Robinson

THE MAN IN THE MIRROR

*"But don't just listen to God's words. You must do what it says.
Otherwise, you are only fooling yourselves. For if you listen to the
word and don't obey, it is like glancing at your face in a mirror.
You see yourself, walk away, and forget what you look like."*
James 1:22-23

James is giving us an analogy of who we are and who God want us to become, and it uncovers our sins that causes us to be disobedient to God. He is saying don't be the ones that hear the word, it sounds good, and it give us a good feeling. Then we turn around and won't do what the word says. God's word teaches us His character. When we read His word, we should be reflecting the character of God.

2 Corinthians 3:18 (Amp) *"And we all, with unveiled face, continually seeing as in a mirror the glory of the Lord, are progressively being transformed into His image from (one degree of) glory to (even more) glory, which comes from the Lord, (who is) the Spirit."*

Genesis 1:27 (KJV) *"So God created man in His own image, in the image of God created Him; male and female created He them."*

Reverend Graylan Richardson

FORMED IN THE MUD, NOT FORSAKEN BY IT

"We are the clay, and You are our potter."
Isaiah 64:8

E ven the messiest situations can shape you for God's purpose. Mud is uncomfortable, but in God's hands, it becomes material for transformation. Let the Potter mold you.

Journal Prompt: What part of your past or present could God be using to prepare you for something greater?

Reverend Dr. Byron L. Benton
Senior Pastor

_____
_____
_____
_____
_____
_____
_____
_____
_____
_____
_____
_____
_____
_____
_____
_____
_____
_____
_____
_____
_____
_____
_____
_____
_____
_____
_____
_____
_____

SEPTEMBER

"Let us not become weary in doing good, for at the proper time we will reap a harvest if we do not give up."

Galatians 6:9

KINGDOM VALUES THAT DISRUPT THE NORM

"Whoever wants to be great must be your servant."
Matthew 20:26

The world values power, but God's kingdom values love and sacrifice. Living in an upside-down way might make you appear foolish to others, but it aligns your heart with Christ.

Journal Prompt: Where can you choose love over power or convenience this week?

Reverend Dr. Byron L. Benton
Senior Pastor

_____
_____
_____
_____
_____
_____
_____
_____
_____
_____
_____
_____
_____
_____
_____
_____
_____
_____
_____
_____
_____
_____
_____
_____
_____
_____

Sing With My Mind?

"For if I pray in an unknown tongue, my spirit prayeth, but my understanding is unfruitful. What is it then? I will pray with the spirit, and I will pray with the understanding also: I will sing with the spirit, and I will sing with the understanding also."
1 Corinthians 14:14-15 (KJV).

U nderstanding is crucial for creating meaningful connections, as highlighted by the Scripture, "in all thy getting, get understanding." Schuman (2023) emphasizes that understanding fosters intimacy and emotional safety. When planning worship songs, it's essential to consider intentionality for positive outcomes. For worship leaders aiming to foster a deeper connection, here are three guiding questions:

1. **Techniques for Intimacy:** What specific methods can worship leaders employ to cultivate a more intimate atmosphere during worship? This could involve variations in song selection, vocal dynamics, and incorporating pauses for reflection.
2. **Discernment of the Holy Spirit:** How can one recognize the presence of the Holy Spirit during worship? Observing congregational engagement, emotional responses, and a sense of peace may indicate the presence of His movement.
3. **Healing Through Singing:** What are practical examples of how singing can serve as a healing mechanism or liberate individuals in a worship context? Testimonies of transformation often highlight the power of collective worship and its ability to bring comfort and restoration.

By reflecting on these questions, worship leaders can enrich their approach, thereby fostering an environment where understanding leads to more profound spiritual encounters.

Schuman, M.(2023). On the importance of being understood. https://www.drmarjorieschuman.com/on-the-importance-of-being- understood-august-2020/

Minister Dr. Lucretia D. Wilson

_____

_____

_____

_____

ADEQUACY IN GOD

*"Not that we are adequate in ourselves to consider anything
as coming from ourselves, but our adequacy is from God."*
2 Corinthians 3:5

I n 2 Corinthians, Paul asks, "who is sufficient" for the task of representing Christ? Our adequacy is always from God. He has already commissioned and sent us. He has given us the Holy Spirit to speak with Christ's power. He keeps His eyes upon us, protecting us as we work for Him. Thus, if we realize that God makes us competent and useful we can overcome our feelings of inadequacy. Serving Him; therefore, requires that we focus on what He can do through us, not on what we can't do by ourselves. In 2 Corinthians, Paul gave God the credit for His accomplishments. While the false teachers boasted of their own power and success, Paul expressed His humility before God. No one can claim to be adequate without God's help. No one is competent to carry out the responsibilities of God's calling in His or her own strength. Without the Holy Spirit's enabling, our natural talent can carry us only so far. As Christ's witnesses, we need the character and special strength that only God gives. Put your trust in the Almighty God, who can do all things but fail.

Minister Sonja Pinckney Rhodes

CHOOSE DIFFERENTLY BECAUSE YOU ARE CHOSEN

"But ye are a chosen generation, a royal priesthood, an holy nation,
a peculiar people; that ye should shew forth the praises of Him who
hath called you out of darkness into His marvellous light: which
in time past were not a people, but are now the people of God:
which had not obtained mercy, but now have obtained mercy."
Peter 2:9-10

W hen you've "been there and done that" enough in life, the popular definition of insanity (continuing to do the same thing and expecting a different outcome) kicks in at some point.

Thanks be to God, that no matter how long it takes, as long as we live and breathe, we have a chance to transition from a "were not" to "are now" people of God! Let us choose today to trust and obey! Our expected end in Christ awaits!

Minister Wallace Hunter

_____
_____
_____
_____
_____
_____
_____
_____
_____
_____
_____
_____
_____
_____
_____
_____
_____
_____
_____
_____
_____
_____
_____

Don't go Back to Egypt

"I am the Lord thy God, which brought thee out of
the land of Egypt, from the house of bondage."
"Ye shall observe to do therefore as the Lord your God
hath commanded you: ye shall not turn aside to the right
hand or to the left. Ye shall walk in all the ways which
the Lord your God hath commanded you, that ye may
live, and that it may be well with you, and that ye may
prolong your days in the land which ye shall possess."
Deuteronomy 5:6, 32-33

E gypt was a physical place of bondage for God's people. However, it can also be a spiritual place and each one of us will experience our own individual Egypts. It could be a habit that we can't break or people we rely on instead of trusting in God. Maybe it's situations we settle for, because we have become discouraged and given up on our dreams.

Know that God wants the best for us here and now, but He requires that we walk according to His way. Egypt can never truly satisfy us, it might make us happy, but it won't give us joy. We may get over financially in an unethical way, but in the end it won't prosper. Jesus is the way out of Egypt and when He delivers us, don't go back, because it's not worth it.

Reverend Leonard Bailey

WAITING

"Yes, my soul, find rest in God; my hope comes from Him."
Psalm 62:5

T he Lord did a great deal of important work in David's life and character during the waiting times, and He does so in you as well. Lord Jesus, you are my hope. I don't mind waiting.

Reverend Gloria Lightfoot

THE RAM IN THE BUSH

Isaac spoke to Abraham His father and said, "My father!" And
He said, "Here I am, my son." Then He said, "Look, the fire
and the wood, but where is the lamb for a burnt offering?"
Genesis 22:7

I n chapter 22 of Genesis, God told Abraham to take His only son, Isaac, to a certain place and sacrifice Him for a burnt offering. Just before Abraham was about to slay Isaac, the angel of the Lord showed up, placed a ram in the thicket, then told Abraham not to touch the lad. How many times in your life you were about to give up, but God sent someone your way just in the nick of time, which gave you a life changing word? I remember when my wife and I went to our bank to take out an equity loan to renovate our home. We had gone through the process of getting a contractor to have the blueprint made. The banker's words were promising that we would be approved for the loan, only to be denied. They said that they would be able to give us a mortgage instead. When I told the contractor we may have put a hold on the renovation and why, He told us about the credit union. We were approved without any hassle. When you faithfully serve God, He will always have a ram in the bush for you.

Roman 8: 28 says, *"And we know that all things work together for good to those who love God, to those who are the called according to His purpose."*

Reverend Graylan Richardson

_____
_____
_____
_____
_____
_____
_____
_____
_____
_____
_____
_____
_____
_____
_____
_____

LAWLESSNESS TO FLAWLESSNESS

"For all have sinned and fall short of the glory of God."
Romans 3:23-26

For all have sinned and fall short of the glory of God, being justified freely by His grace through the redemption that is in Christ Jesus, whom God set forth *as* a propitiation by His blood, through faith, to demonstrate His righteousness, because in His forbearance, God had passed over the sins that were previously committed, to demonstrate at the present time His righteousness, that He might be just and the justifier of the one who has faith in Jesus.

We all have fallen short, and are born as sinners. Yet, hope remains. Through grace, we are redeemed, not through our own merit. The gift of salvation washes away our flaws, making us flawless. These 5 keys are the essence to Christian's faith:

1. **Human Imperfection:** Acknowledges that no one is without sin or flaw and recognizes the inherent limitations of human nature.
2. **Divine Grace:** Emphasizes the concept of God's unmerited favor and highlights that salvation is a gift, not something earned through good deeds.
3. **Redemption and Transformation:** Describes the process of spiritual renewal and cleansing and asserts that through faith in Christ, individuals can be made new.
4. **Divine Perfection:** Asserts that God sees believers as perfect, despite their imperfections and highlights the transformative power of God's love.
5. **Freedom in Christ:** Encourages readers to embrace the freedom that comes from accepting God's grace and calls for a life lived in accordance with God's will.

Minister Rosalyn Brown

_____

_____

_____

_____

_____

_____

_____

Your Time Is Today

"There is a time for everything, and a season
for every activity under the heavens."
Ecclesiastes 3:1

You are exactly where you need to be. The problem isn't your place; it's your timing. We often struggle when we rush ahead or hold on too long, forgetting that every season has a purpose. Each moment—whether a problem, celebration, or waiting period—carries a lesson and a blessing. When you focus on this season, instead of wishing for the next, you position yourself to experience its full glory. What if this is the season to grow, heal, or prepare? What if this is the time to reap the reward of seeds you've already planted? God's timing is perfect, and so is His plan for you. Your potential is limitless, and opportunities abound in every season. Instead of asking, "Why now?" ask, "What can I learn? How can I grow?" Your time isn't coming—it's here. Today's Declaration: I declare that I will embrace this season with faith and purpose. I am in the right place, and my time is now. Today's Challenge: Reflect on where you are today. Write down one opportunity you can seize or one lesson you can learn in this season. Trust that God's timing is preparing you for something greater.

Reverend Randy Adkins Jr.

A MOTHER LOVINGLY STANDS BY

*"My God, my God, why have you forsaken me? Why are you
so far from saving me, so far from my cries of anguish?"*
Psalm 22: 1-8

I was there when they crucified my **Son** and nailed Him to the tree. I witnessed them pierce His side as the sun refused to shine. I recalled bringing my infant **Son** to the temple for dedication, where Simeon took Him and blessed Him, saying, "A sword shall pierce through thy own soul also." I didn't know then that I would experience both darkness and daylight as my firstborn fulfilled His mission.

My heart was heavy as I stood beneath the rugged cross, witnessing the degradation, desolation, and death of the one I loved so deeply. I had to endure the blasphemies and lies of the priests and the crowd against my **Son**. My sorrow was immense, but I stayed so my **Son** would know I would not desert Him as many of His disciples had done. The pain of seeing my innocent **Son** branded a criminal, hung between two thieves, was unbearable. Yet, I found courage and faith, believing it was part of a divine order that called me to remain at the cross to receive my **Son's** parting blessing.

In His agony, He thought of me enough to entrust me to John, the disciple He loved.

According to scripture, the last glimpse of Mary is heartwarming; she stands among believers in the upper chamber (Acts 1:12-14). Her **Son** is alive forevermore, and life has changed for her. She takes her place among those waiting for the Holy Spirit to equip them for the start of the Christian Community.

Reverend Dr. Brenda Joyce Stallings

MISERY LOVES COMPANY

"Then it says, 'I will return to the person I came from.' So, it returns and finds its former home empty, swept, and in order."
Matthew 12:44 NLT

M atthew communicates a snapshot of internal emptiness and the hazards of vulnerability after a spiritual cleaning. Removing negative influences or habits must include filling the space with Godly positivity to mitigate the return of negativity. Without a proactive habit that cultivates spiritual growth and maturity, the clean inner being becomes a dwelling place for old, ungodly spirits to live comfortably. Old habits resurface along with worse habits because misery loves company.

To mitigate the risk of Mr. Misery having company at the expense of the spiritually cleansed vessel, a believer must secure its clean temple with prayer, reading the Scriptures, and surrounding oneself with God-fearing disciples of Christ. Lasting change and spiritual maturity require vigilance in spiritual, emotional, and physical areas of one's life.

A moving weekly sermon helps in the transformative process to keep one's body occupied with Godly material. Daily studies of Scriptures support a consistent lifestyle. Mr. Misery will have no occupancy nor room to invite company to invade your temple of the Holy Ghost, which is your body. Fill your life with God-centered songs and fellowship with other like-minded believers. What will you do to maintain positive changes in your life? Take the initiative to maintain your body as a temple of the Holy Ghost.

Dr. Pamela Gay

START SMALL

*Then He said, "What is the kingdom of God like? And to
what shall I compare it? It is like a mustard seed, which a
man took and put in His garden; and it grew and became a
large tree, and the birds of the air nested in its branches."*
Luke 13:18-19

I was talking to a friend the other day who has been saved about a year. This person felt that they were moving too slowly in their walk with Christ. I shared this scripture with them to encourage them.

The world encourages quick and explosive growth. Mark Zuckerberg, the founder and CEO of Facebook, famously told His staff to "Move fast and break things." Most jobs are looking for quick self-starters with 5 years of experience to hire. It seems like no matter the size of our order, we're looking at our watch if the people at our favorite fast food spot take more than a few minutes.

This isn't how Jesus describes His kingdom. His Kingdom starts with the "smallest" people. The poor, the marginalized, the sick, the disabled, and the uneducated were all among the people Jesus brought His kingdom to first.

If you feel like the work you're doing for Christ is too small to matter, you need to understand that Jesus works in the small. Jesus can take the mustard seed of faith you had and give you eternal life. What else can He do with the faith that you have now?

Minister Kon Robinson

JOY THAT TESTIFIES

"They broke bread in their homes and ate together
with glad and sincere hearts, praising God and
enjoying the favor of all the people."
Acts 2:46–47

There's a kind of joy that can't be manufactured — it's born in community, shaped by gratitude, and sustained by worship. The believers in Acts didn't just gather in temples — they opened their homes and hearts. Their joy wasn't circumstantial; it flowed from sincerity, unity, and the presence of God in their midst. And here's the beautiful part: their joy became their witness. People *noticed*. The way they loved, served, and rejoiced together drew others in — and the Lord added to their number daily.

Today, in a world hungry for authenticity, joy rooted in Jesus still draws hearts. It's not about pretending life is perfect, but about living with deep gratitude and honest faith. Let your joy speak. Let your praise rise in your home, not just at church. Share a meal and a testimony. Let people see that your faith is not just words — it's a lived experience marked by gladness and sincerity. What if your joy is someone else's open door to Christ?

Let's live so that our lives sing the gospel before we ever say a word.

Minister Sonja Pinckney Rhodes

Are You Still Thirsty? Here's The Living Water

"Jesus answered, "Everyone who drinks this water will be thirsty again, 14 but whoever drinks the water I give them will never thirst. Indeed, the water I give them will become in them a spring of water welling up to eternal life."
John 4: 13

The slogan Quench Your Thirst was made popular by Gatorade. It means to stop being thirsty. Well, God's words told us that "we for all have sinned and fall short of the glory of God" (Romans 3:23). Sins were those times when we felt "thirsty," so we decided to quench our thirst by responding in the flesh. Just like the Samaritan woman in the text, we continued to draw from "that well." We continued to be thirsty because the act of sin was a resource and not the source of healing. The act became a habit, a cover-up, a worry, or an addiction. Jesus wanted to quench the thirst of the Samaritan woman. So, He was intentional in meeting with her at the well. God wants to meet with you as well. Are you still thirsty? You are that special to Him and He is waiting at the well for you too. Try Jesus as the Source of healing to help you to overcome the "ways of life." Drink from His beautiful spring that will never run dry." He is the Living Water.

Minister Dr. Nathalina Rogers-Tolbert

FAITHFUL THROUGH THE FOG

"Let us hold unswervingly to the hope we
profess, for He who promised is faithful."
Hebrews 10:23

Today, some of us may feel like we're moving through fog - uncertain, weary, and waiting for clarity. Life's disappointments, delays, and detours can sometimes make us question if what we're hoping for will ever come to pass. But this morning, don't let the fog make you forget God's faithfulness.

Hebrews 10:23 calls us to *hold unswervingly* - that means with a tight, unwavering grip - to the hope we profess. Why? Because He who promised is faithful. The faithfulness of God is not determined by how we feel or what we see, but by who He is. He has a perfect track record. He's never failed, and He won't start with you.

Hope isn't just wishful thinking; it's confidence in God's character. It's choosing to believe, even in silence, that God is good, and He's not finished yet. You're still in the waiting room of life. Faithfulness in the waiting proves your trust in the One who holds time in His hands.

Your season of fulfillment is coming. God sees you He loves you. He is faithful to complete what He started in you.

Lord, we thank You this morning for being a faithful God. Even when we can't trace Your hand, we trust Your heart. Help us to remain faithful while we wait - faithful in our walk, faithful in our worship, and faithful in our hope. Give us strength and remind us that You're working everything together for our good. In Jesus' name, Amen.

Minister Rhulaunda Donald

_____
_____
_____
_____
_____
_____
_____
_____
_____
_____
_____

A FRESH ANOINTING

"The anointing you received from Him remains in you."
1 John 2:27

S ometimes, life can feel like a routine—same things, day after day. We go through the motions, but deep down, we might feel drained or disconnected from our purpose. But when we turn to Christ, He offers us something special: a fresh anointing.

Anointing in the Bible is a symbol of God's power and presence. It's a spiritual blessing that empowers us to do what we cannot do on our own. In 1 John 2:27, it says, *"The anointing you received from Him remains in you..."* This means that when we accept Jesus into our lives, His Spirit is with us, equipping us with new strength, wisdom, and purpose.

A fresh anointing in Christ doesn't mean everything will be easy, but it does mean that God gives us the strength to rise above challenges. When we invite Him into our lives daily, He fills us with His Spirit and empowers us to live with purpose and joy.

Minister Sonja Pinckney Rhodes

WOUNDED PART 2

"Seek the Lord while He may be found;
Call upon Him while He is near."
Isaiah 55:6

When we're wounded, God is so gracious and abounding in love, He picks us up and restores us. He helps us to feel spiritually whole again. How does He do this? I believe the Holy Spirit of the living God tugs at our hearts, causing us to cry out to Him. Causing us to seek His face in prayer. Sometimes God allows certain things to happen in our lives to get our attention so that we will pray. We will reach for the Bible again; and we will not forsake the assembling of ourselves with other saints, Hebrews 10:25 We will also return to church worship services.

We must cry out to God; He patiently awaits our return.

"For I am poor and needy, and my heart is wounded within me." Psalm 109:22. God provides the healing that we need when we are spiritually wounded. He comforts us when we call on Him. When we do not have that intimacy with God through prayer, reading His Word and fellowship with the saints, we become spiritually inept, sick and weak. Just as depriving ourselves of proper nourishment and nutrition would result in sickness or disease in our physical bodies, depriving our spirit man of proper nourishment causes sickness within our spirits as well.

He restoreth my soul, my cup runneth over. If you are feeling weak spiritually, call on Jesus.

Reverend Brenda Smalls-Robinson

_____
_____
_____
_____
_____
_____
_____
_____
_____
_____
_____
_____
_____

OCTOBER

*"The Lord directs the steps of the godly. He delights in
every detail of their lives. Though they stumble, they
will never fall, for the Lord holds them by the hand."*

Psalm 37:23–24

Faithfulness Doesn't Exempt You From Mud

"Save me, God. I am sinking deep in the mud..."
Psalm 69:1-2

Sometimes, you're stuck not because of sin, but because of righteousness. David suffered not just from failure, but from faithfulness. Being zealous for God can still invite criticism or rejection — but God sees, hears, and honors your endurance.

Journal Prompt: Have you experienced hardship while trying to do the right thing? How did you respond?

Reverend Dr. Byron L. Benton
Senior Pastor

WORKING FOR THE KINGDOM OF GOD

*"Therefore, my beloved brethren, be steadfast,
immoveable, always abounding in the work of the Lord,
knowing that your labor is not in vain in the Lord."*
1 Corinthians 15:58

One of my younger brothers is a pastor of a small church in Mt. Pleasant. I remember once, there were two deaths in the community back-to-back and in one week He officiated over two funerals. I attended both funerals. I have never attended two funerals in one week in my entire life.

Whatever you have in your heart to do for the Lord, do it. Do not hesitate. Do not procrastinate. Do it today! Tomorrow is not promised to any of us.

Jesus said in **John 9:4 – NKJV –** *"I must work the works of Him who sent Me while it is day; the night is coming when no one can work."*

Do something for the furtherance of the kingdom of God *this* day; and let's continue to pray one for another.

Reverend Brenda Smalls-Robinson

KNOW GOD FOR YOURSELVES

"That I may know Him, and the power of His resurrection."
Philippians 3: 10

A s Christians, the Lord wants to use us to lead people into a relationship with Him. And when we think of how good the Lord has been to us and where He has brought us from, we should desire that all people would come to know Jesus Christ as their Lord and Savior.

The main idea is to know God, to be known by God and to make God known that we may better proclaim the gospel of Jesus Christ. **Paul** says that "His heart belongs to God, to know Him is the power of the resurrection and the fellowship of His suffering." Paul is demonstrating that we should live our lives in such a way that the world knows that we are not of the world, because we have been called **out of the world** by a risen Savior.

It is imperative to believe that knowing God is more than just talking to God, but we must be a living **protype** of whom God is. It is more than just having a **single** encounter with God. We need to know the **power** of His resurrection and that one day when this life is over; we shall rise again with Him and receive that mansion in heaven that God declares in John 14. But not just for ourselves, but that our families would know Him, as well.

Minister Sonja Pinckney Rhodes

THE IMPORTANCE OF OUR PRAYERS

"Rejoice evermore. Pray without ceasing. In everything give thanks: for this is the will of God in Christ Jesus concerning you."
1 Thessalonians 5:16-18

Our prayers are powerful tools that connect us with the Almighty. They have the potential to bring about miraculous changes and empower us. Approaching God authentically and freedom from selfish motives are essential. As Numbers 23:19 reminds us, God is faithful to His promises, and we should boldly remind Him of those promises in our prayers. While God already knows our needs, we are encouraged to ask in faith, trusting in His promises. Maintain a constant connection with God through continual prayer, following His guidance and avoiding vain repetitions. Trust in His Word, knowing that our prayers are alive and powerful, guaranteed to fulfill their purpose. So let us unite in prayer, confident that God's blessings will exceed our understanding. Remember the examples of faithful figures like Joseph, Joshua, Esther, and Hannah, who demonstrate the power of prayer. If blessings seem delayed, it may be due to the disobedience of others, so continue to pray purposefully. As you meditate on today's scriptures, reflect on the following: 1) Specific examples of God's promises, 2) Ways to connect with God daily through prayer, and 3) Practical steps to take if you feel your prayers are unanswered. Take time to discern what God is saying to you right now.

Minister Dr. Lucretia D. Wilson

Anchor Of Hope

"We have this hope as an anchor for the soul, firm and secure. It enters the inner sanctuary behind the curtain."
Hebrews 6:19

The Lord has promised never to leave or forsake You. He has a plan for your life, and He will be the Anchor that keeps you steady through every storm. Jesus, Thank You for being my hope.

Reverend Gloria Lightfoot

STIR OR COVER

"Hatred stirs up conflict, but love covers over all wrongs."
Proverbs 10:12

Every day, we face a choice: to stir or to cover. Stirring arises from hatred — keeping offenses alive, seeking revenge, or fueling conflict. But what does it achieve? Stirring only prolongs pain, deepens wounds, and perpetuates division. Love, however, takes a higher road. Love covers — not to ignore wrongs but to forgive, release, and let go. Covering doesn't mean weakness; it means choosing peace over pride. Love gives even when it hurts, offering grace where resentment could take root. When you choose to cover, you choose freedom. You release the bitterness that binds you and allow God's peace to flow through you. Covering wrongs doesn't just bless others; it transforms your own heart, filling it with clarity, wholeness, and compassion. Today's Declaration: I choose to cover, not stir. I release all thoughts of wrongdoing, rejection, or incompleteness. I declare God's blessings of peace, kindness, and love over my life. Today's Challenge: Reflect on someone who has wronged you. Instead of stirring up conflict, ask God for the strength to cover the situation with love. Forgive, let go, and embrace the freedom that comes with His peace.

Reverend Randy Adkins Jr.

A PERFECT PRAYER PARTNER

*"Who then will condemn us?" No one—for Christ Jesus
died for us and was raised to life for us, Jesus is at the
right hand of God and is also interceding for you."*
Romans 8:34 declares

N ow, that's good news. Jesus Christ is the "perfect prayer
partner," the perfect friend who intercedes for you with
immeasurable grace, love, kindness, and perseverance. His
prayers are beautiful, no, they are breathtaking, beyond prayers you
could never image or think.

When you know that there is a friend praying for you with compassion
and God-given insight, it is like heaven touching earth. Wow!

Yes, there are times you may struggle with words and feelings of
inadequacies, but Jesus taught His followers to always pray and not
give-up. Here's why. It is He, Jesus, who searches the heart of a man and
knows the mind of the Holy Spirit to make intercession for you according
to the will of God. Now, you know with certainty that the perfect prayer
partner. Will never leave you to pray alone. So, get excited my brothers
and sisters. Begin to experience Jesus Christ, as your "perfect prayer
partner," inviting Him and the Holy Spirit to continue praying for you.

Minister Janet Williams-Johnson

You Are What You Eat!

"But Jesus answered Him, saying, "It is written, 'Man shall not live by bread alone, but by every word of God."
Luke 4:4

Like most children, one of my favorite things to eat growing up was peanut butter and jelly sandwiches. I would have eaten them every day if I could! While peanut butter has plenty of protein, it's also high in fat and does not provide enough of the vitamins and minerals our bodies need to stay healthy.

As adults, we understand that our spiritual well-being is even more important than our physical health. And just as our bodies can't survive on peanut butter and jelly alone, neither can our spirits. The sandwich may sustain our physical body, but it does nothing for our spirit—and if our spiritual self does not receive proper nourishment, it too will weaken and starve.

Our well-being is shaped not only by what we consume physically but also by what we take into our hearts and what we allow to come out of our mouths. This is what ultimately shapes our lives.

Each day, we should ask the Holy Spirit to be our guide, our speech writer, and to give us our daily bread!

Reverend Valarie Pritchard

PRAISE GOD ANYHOW

"Make a joyful noise unto the Lord, all ye lands."
Psalm 100

A s we go through our daily routines, sometimes as if We have no reason for praising God. Our petitions seem to be going unanswered; our problems continue to grow with no solutions in our sight, our health is getting worse, our bills are going unpaid- so, what do we have to praise God for? We praise God because He is worthy to be praised. We praise God because He loved us so much that He sent His Son to die for us. We praise God because He is God.

Yes, we all go through these dry periods, periods of time when one or more of the problems listed above seem to haunt us. But God's word tells us to stand steadfast in faith knowing that these same struggles are being experienced by many others. He has promised us that if we place our cares upon Him, He will take care of us. It is easier to say, than to do. However, give God a chance to prove that His word is true. Your help may not come today, tomorrow or the next day but believe the word of God - help will come.

God loves to be praised. God should be praised. God is the only one worthy of praise. We will praise Him for being God, for never changing, for His miracles, His steadfastness, and for sending His Son, Jesus. Also, for the death and resurrection of Jesus, for His saving blood, for allowing His Holy Spirit to dwell within us. We will praise Him because He is the great I Am.

The God above all God's
Because He cares for us
Because He loves us
Because we love Him!!!
Everyday is praise day.

Reverend Dr. Brenda Joyce Stalling

RENEWAL

"That you put off concerning the former conversation the old man,
which is corrupt according to the deceitful lusts; and be renewed
in the spirit of your mind; and that you put on the new man,
which after God is created in righteousness and true holiness."
Ephesians 4:22 – 24

R enewal is what happens when God pours out His Spirit on His people. And it's when He is free to work powerfully in and through us to show the world how **real** and **mighty** and **good** Jesus is.

God renews our hearts, our minds, our souls and our strength. To do this, the book of Ephesians says to put off your old self, which belongs to your former manner of life, and is corrupt through deceitful desires, and to be renewed in the spirit of your **minds**, and to put on the new self, created after the likeness of God in true righteousness and holiness.

We should be able to see a difference between Christians and non-Christians because of the way Christians live. Paul tells the Ephesians to leave behind the old life of sin now that they are followers of Christ. Living the Christian life is a process. Although we have a new nature, we don't automatically have all good thoughts and attitudes when we become new people in Christ. But if we keep listening to God, and obeying Him, we will be changing all the time. As you look over the last year, do you see a process of change for the better in your thoughts, attitudes, and actions? Although change may be slow, it is necessary, and it only comes about if you surrender to and trust God to change you.

Minister Sonja Pinckney Rhodes

_____
_____
_____
_____
_____
_____
_____
_____
_____
_____
_____
_____
_____

PERFECTION IN JESUS

"But He said to me, 'My grace is sufficient for you,
for my power is made perfect in weakness."
2 Corinthians 12:9

W hen I came to Mount Moriah, I was searching for a church home, not facing a terminal illness, but simply hurting and confused. I couldn't understand how a loving God would ask nothing more than my acceptance of His love. I was focused on my imperfections and couldn't rest in the perfection that comes from embracing our weaknesses.

Jesus tells us that His strength is made perfect in our weakness. I often felt like Uzzah, trying to steady the ark, thinking I needed to support a foundation already built on the rock of faith. I shared God's love but was afraid to receive it for myself. Subconsciously, I thought I had to fix myself before God could love me.

Through the Word preached at Mount Moriah, I began to understand that I didn't have to achieve righteousness on my own. I could receive it from Jesus, who was sent to provide it. John 7:38 says, *"Whoever believes in me, as Scripture has said, rivers of living water will flow from within them."* I drank deeply from that well and found healing. Isaiah 53:1 asks, *"Who hath believed our report? And to whom is the arm of the Lord revealed?"* I've seen the arm of the Lord revealed in my life through Jesus Christ.

Reverend Thomas Robinson

No Other Way

"Dear friends, although I was very eager to write to you about the salvation we share, I felt compelled to write and urge you to contend for the faith that was once for all entrusted to God's holy people. For certain individuals whose condemnation was written aboutlong ago have secretly slipped in among you. They are ungodly people, who pervert the grace of our God into a license for immorality and deny Jesus Christ our only Sovereign and Lord."

Jude 1: 3-4

Jude urges us to contend for the faith that was once and for all given to us. Any person, religion or ideology that teaches that there is any other way for salvation is a false doctrine. God has already made the only way to salvation and there is no other way to be reconciled to God. *"Jesus is the way the truth and the life, No one can come to the father except through Him (John 14:6)."*

Reverend Leonard Bailey

No Longer Condemned

"Therefore, if anyone is in Christ, the new creation
has come:[a] The old has gone, the new is here!"
2 Corinthians 5:17

A re you feeling secure in who you are in God through Christ Jesus? There is no reason you should not be! When you accepted Jesus Christ as your Lord and Savior by faith, His Holy Spirit indwelled you. God says to you, *"Therefore, if anyone is in Christ, He is a new creation; the old has passed away, and see, the new has come (2 Cor. 5:17, CSB)."*

No longer condemn! Speak these words out loud to yourself, and then tell God thank you for His saving grace and mercy towards you!

Guess what? You and I are eternally secure in Christ! Condemned is not who we are because we have placed our faith in God through Christ Jesus, and our sins are forgiven. The old life we lived prior to salvation is obsolete, and now we live and walk in the newness of our salvation in Christ Jesus.

Once saved, we will still stumble, we will struggle, we will experience disappointments, pain, and sometimes hardships, but we are not condemned according to God's Word. The question we must ask ourselves is "whose report are we going to believe?" The Word of God or the adversary?

God said, "No condemnation for those who are in Christ Jesus." Whose report have you chosen to believe? I hope you will join me in saying that you also chose to "believe the report of the Lord!" No longer condemned! Glory to Your name Lord! Thank you, Jesus!

Minister Debra Aiken

LIGHTS WERE MADE TO SHINE

"Let your light so shine before men, that they may see your good works, and glorify your Father which is in heaven."
Matthew 5:16

J esus was the chosen to come to earth to die for our sins. Because of Him, we can do all things through Him. You were chosen, by God, to be a member of His kingdom family. No, you did not sign up or decide to take a membership card. But the greatest joy was that He chose you to represent Him which made you special in His eyes. You were one of His greatest masterpieces that He took delight in seeing shine for His glory. Be encouraged to let your light of love, kindness, faithfulness, gifts, and talents shine for the Lord. You were created to worship Him in spirit and truth. "This Little Light of Mine, I'm Going to Let it Shine. Let it shine, Let it shine, Let it shine." Let His spirit overflow as you serve Him by shining your light bright daily in all you do.

Minister Dr. Nathalina Rogers-Tolbert

THE BENEFITS OF TRUSTING

"Trust in the Lord and do good; dwell in the
land and cultivate faithfulness.
Psalm 37:3

T rust is a simple word, yet it carries a vast meaning. Living out this meaning can lead to heartaches, pain, misery, strife, and blessings. The key to positive outcomes lies in depending on the right source. Are you in the midst of a decision and in need of guidance? Remember that a compass provides directions to prevent you from getting lost. It also assists with navigation and orientation by showing the cardinal directions. The collection of Proverbs, primarily attributed to King Solomon, offers wise counsel, especially in Proverbs 3:5-6a: *"Trust in and rely confidently on the Lord with all your heart and do not rely on your own insight or understanding. In all your ways, know and acknowledge and recognize Him, and He will make your paths straight and smooth [removing obstacles that block your way]. Do not be wise in your own eyes (AMP Version)."* Practicing trust according to scripture encourages wisdom and sound decision-making. Viewing your choices through the lens of the Holy One will never steer you wrong. You will feel guided, knowing you are on the right path — the true benefits of trusting a faithful and wise God.

Minister Dr. Lucretia D. Wilson

Forgiveness: The Path That Leads To Love

*"Therefore, I tell you, her many sins have been
forgiven—as her great love has shown. But
whoever has been forgiven little loves little."*
Luke 7:47

Climbing a mountain is no easy task, it takes skill, great physical and mental endurance, and bravery. Gravity is not your friend, which means the more weight you carry up the mountain the harder this task becomes. If a mountain climber was given an extra 1000 pounds, in addition to the weight they already must carry, the task of climbing a mountain would be extremely hard, and impossible for most. When we choose not to forgive, we become like mountain climbers carrying heavy weights. We cannot expect for God to elevate us to the next level of our mountain when we are carrying the heavy burden of unforgiveness. Forgiveness at times is not an easy thing to do, especially when the ones we need to forgive have hurt us deeply and left us broken-hearted. The path that leads to forgiveness, is often a hard route to find, but Jesus Christ teaches us that if we allow love to be our guide, it will lead us to a place where we can dispose of the bitter, barrier that obstructs us from giving and receiving the love that Christ has shown us when He forgives us for our sins. Friends we should no longer allow the weight of not forgiving others to prevent us from moving closer to God.

Minister Tristan Simmons

TURBULENT SEASONS

"To everything there is a season, A time for
every purpose under heaven."
Ecclesiastes 3:1

T here is a time for everything, and that includes times of hardship. Even in a toxic political season, when life feels difficult, remember that challenges are not permanent. Just as surely as the sun sets each night, tough times will eventually give way to brighter days. Hold onto hope and keep praying, trusting, and believing that God will see you through. Keep moving forward, one day at a time. All seasons shall pass. When faced with difficult times, remember these thoughts:

- The power of hope: Hope is a powerful emotion that can help us get through tough times. When we hold onto hope, we are more likely to find the strength to keep going.
- The importance of perseverance: Even when things are tough, it's important to keep moving forward. One step at a time, we can overcome any challenge.
- The impermanence of suffering: Suffering is not permanent. Just as surely as the sun rises each morning, brighter days will come.

Minister Rosalyn Brown

GRACE THAT WASHES DEEP STAINS

"If we confess our sins, He is faithful and just to forgive us..."
1 John 1:9

No matter how muddy our mistakes, God's grace goes deeper. David's life teaches us that confession is not defeat—it's the beginning of restoration. When we bring our mess honestly to God, He doesn't recoil; He redeems. There is no stain too stubborn for the blood of Jesus.

Journal Prompt: What area of your life needs God's cleansing grace today?

Reverend Dr. Byron L. Benton
Senior Pastor

NOVEMBER

"Give thanks in all circumstances;
for this is God's will for you in Christ Jesus."

1 Thessalonians 5:18

CHOSEN WHILE FLAWED

"He will rejoice over you with gladness."
Zephaniah 3:17

G od doesn't wait for perfection — He chooses you now, flaws and all. His love isn't based on merit, but on His mercy. This truth humbles us and fuels gratitude.

Journal Prompt: How does knowing you are chosen — even in weakness — impact the way you see yourself today?

Reverend Dr. Byron L. Benton
Senior Pastor

_____
_____
_____
_____
_____
_____
_____
_____
_____
_____
_____
_____
_____
_____
_____
_____
_____
_____
_____
_____
_____
_____
_____
_____
_____

He Knows The Plans

"For I know the thoughts that I think toward you, saith the Lord,
thoughts of peace, and not of evil, to give you an expected end."
Jeremiah 29:11

W e all feel inspired by a leader who pushes us to move forward, someone who believes we can accomplish the tasks they give us and who supports us throughout the journey. God is that kind of leader. He knows what the future holds, and His plans for us are good and filled with hope. He created the universe, and He has a specific plan for every person on Earth. He has already set everything in motion to ensure you have a bright future.

As long as God, who knows what's coming, sets our goals and walks with us as we carry out His mission, we can have endless hope. Our future is secure, but that doesn't mean we won't face pain, suffering, or challenges; it means God will guide us through to a wonderful ending.

Minister Sonja Pinckney Rhodes

GOD'S DIRECTIONS

"Therefore, everyone who hears these words of mine and puts them into practice is like a wise man who built His house on the rock. The rain came down, the streams rose, and the winds blew and beat against that house; yet it did not fall, because it had its foundation on the rock. But everyone who hears these words of mine and does not put them into practice is like a foolish man who built His house on sand. The rain came down, the streams rose, and the winds blew and beat against that house, and it fell with a great crash."
Matthew 7:24-27

When baking a cake, there are steps that must be followed in order for the cake to turn out as desired. Skipping steps or leaving out a necessary ingredient could turn out disastrous. It could cause the cake to fall instead of rising. Adding too much of any ingredient could also cause problems, making the cake inedible.

We tend to follow directions closely when making a cake because we want it to turn out as desired. Step by step, we meticulously follow the instructions. What happens when God gives us directions for our lives? How much more important is it to follow His directions? Often, He tells us to add qualities to our lives like faith, hope and love while leaving out things like anger, jealousy and bitterness. Too much or too little can interfere with the results God intends to achieve in or through us.

Pay close attention to the directions you receive from God. They shape who and what you become!

Reverend Valarie Pritchard

COME BEFORE WINTER

*"Do your best to come before winter, Eubulus greets
you, Puden, Linus, Claudia, and all the brethren."*
2 Timothy 4: 9-21

There have been times when we intend to do something like visit a sick friend at home or in the hospital or make a phone call to someone we have not seen or heard from in a while. We hear a small voice that tells us to make that call, make that visit, send a card-just thinking about you and then later we find we should have acted but didn't; we were too late. Our friend or loved one is no longer with us. Though our intentions were great, they are now too late for what we should have and could have done. The Lord has taken them on to glory land and now there is a void in our spirits. If only we had listened to that still small voice, the voice of the Lord. Tomorrow is not promised to any of us. "Please come before winter."

Reverend Samuel Fennoy

Veterans Day Honoring Those Who Serve

*"Greater love has no one than this: to lay
down one's own life for one's friends."*
John 15:13

T he verse highlights the profound selflessness and unwavering sacrifice that countless veterans exemplify through their service to the nation. Their actions stand as a testament to a deep-rooted commitment and unparalleled bravery, reflecting the dedication required to protect and serve not only their country but also the values of freedom and justice for all. These noble qualities echo the profound love and sacrifice that Jesus demonstrated at the cross for the sake of humanity, offering hope and redemption.

As we embark on this day, let us take a moment to reflect on the immense gratitude we owe to those who have served. Their sacrifices provide us with blessings and opportunities we often take for granted. May we be inspired by their courage and sincerely appreciate the grace and mercies that come to us through the sacrifices of others, fostering a sense of community and responsibility toward those who continue to serve and protect.

Reverend Ocie Gay
U.S Army Retired
Purple Heart Recipient

ALL THINGS WORK TOGETHER

"And we know that in all things God works for the good of those who love Him, who have been called according to His purpose."
Romans 8:28

I t's hard to see the "good" when life feels broken. But God isn't finished. Romans 8:28 declares that "in all things" — not just the wins, but also the disappointments — God is working. Your current struggle is not wasted. God is the ultimate Author, weaving every chapter together for a greater good you may not yet see. This moment may be full of uncertainty, but it is not without purpose. Even your delay has direction. When we surrender our narrative to God, He brings clarity out of confusion and beauty from brokenness. You are still in His hands. And though today may feel like a setback, trust that it's part of your setup for something greater. Speak life. Choose hope. God's purpose still stands.

Dr. Da'rrell Ravenell

DARE TO EXPECT MORE

"Now to Him who is able to do exceedingly abundantly above all that we ask or think, according to the power that works in us."
Ephesians 3:20

Why is it easier to expect disappointment than to hope for the miraculous? Maybe it's the pain of past letdowns. Maybe it's fear disguised as realism. Or maybe, over time, we've learned to protect our hearts by shrinking our expectations. In doing so, we subtly train ourselves to anticipate lack instead of overflow — and miss the joy of living in hopeful faith. But faith wasn't meant to play it safe.

Ephesians 3:20 reminds us that the God we serve is not limited by what we've seen, lost, or feared. His power is at work in us, not just around us. He doesn't deal in scraps or just-enough answers. He deals in *exceedingly, abundantly, and above.*

He is able to do *immeasurably more* — not just slightly more, or possibly more — but *beyond what we ask or imagine.* That means our boldest prayers, our biggest dreams, and our secret longings are only starting points for what God *can* and *wants* to do.

Great expectations are signs of faith. They show that we believe God is not only able, but willing — and actively working for our good. They reflect trust in His timing, His wisdom, and His heart.

So today, resist the urge to expect the worst. Expect to be amazed. Normalize hope. And when fear whispers, "What if it doesn't happen?" let faith respond, "But what if it does — and it's even better than I imagined?"

Pray big. Hope deeply. Imagine freely. God is preparing to exceed even your boldest prayer.

Minister Rhulaunda Donald

There Is A Thief Among Us

*"For I know the thoughts that I think toward you, says the Lord,
thoughts of peace and not of evil, to give you a future and a hope."*
Jeremiah 29:11

God has good thoughts for us. He offers us a future of hope, prosperity, and peace. On the other hand, there is a thief that is among us that wants to rob us of all the things that God has promised us.

The thief that is among us is the devil, but we have a Protector in the Holy Spirit from the enemy. John 10:10 says *"The thief does not come except to steal, and to kill, and to destroy. I have come that they may have life, and that they may have it more abundantly."* God offers abundant blessings. We can embrace the fullness of life, knowing we are deserving of God's blessings. We must let go of fear and ask the Holy Spirit to protect us from physical and spiritual danger.

Minister Rosalyn Brown

GIVE YOUR CARES TO GOD

*"Come to me, all you who are weary and
burdened , and I will give you rest."*
Matthew 11:28

J oseph M. Scriven's song, "What A Friend We Have In Jesus," assures us that we can take all our burdens to the Lord in prayer. Often, however, we forfeit our peace and endure needless pain instead of accepting Jesus' invitation to bring our struggles to Him. He doesn't ask us to fix ourselves first; He simply says, "Come to Me." What a blessing it is to know that God promises us rest—not just physical rest, but rest for our weary hearts and souls. We can find this rest by praying and leaving our cares at Jesus' feet, as God is willing to bear it all.

The burdens we carry are not just physical; they also include emotional stress, financial hardships, and spiritual doubts—fear, guilt, and exhaustion from trying to manage everything alone. Jesus has already taken on the greatest burden of sin for us, allowing us to release our struggles into His care. He invites us to cast every burden upon Him, and in return, we discover freedom, peace, and true rest.

Today, I choose to let go of my worries and trust that Christ will sustain us. May we remember that He offers a yoke that is light and filled with grace. In Him, we will find the rest we need to navigate life's challenges, embracing the promise of renewal and strength that comes from trusting in His love.

Reverend Julette M. Scott

THE ARMOR OF GOD

"Finally, my brethren, be strong in the Lord,
and in the power of His might."
Ephesians 6:10 – 18

The Apostle Paul encourages us to be strong in our faith and to prepare ourselves for the challenges we face in life. This passage describes the "armor of God," a powerful metaphor that helps us understand how to protect ourselves spiritually. First, Paul tells us to be strong in the Lord. This means relying on God's strength rather than our own. When we face difficulties — whether they are personal struggles, peer pressure, or emotional challenges — it's important to remember that we can ask God for help. He is always there to support us.

Next, Paul describes various pieces of armor: the belt of truth, the breastplate of righteousness, shoes of peace, the shield of faith, the helmet of salvation, and the sword of the Spirit. Each piece symbolizes an important aspect of our faith. For example, the belt of truth reminds us to be honest and to seek the truth in our lives. The shield of faith helps us defend against negativity and doubt.

Wearing this armor means preparing ourselves for spiritual battles. It encourages us to stand firm in our beliefs, to pray regularly, and to stay connected with others who share our faith. By doing so, we can face challenges with confidence and resilience.

In conclusion, Ephesians 6:10-18 teaches us that we are not alone in our struggles. With God's armor, we can stand strong, protect ourselves, and inspire others to do the same.

Minister Sonja Pinckney Rhodes

WATCH YOUR MOUTH

"But no human being can tame the tongue. It is a restless evil, full of deadly poison. With the tongue we praise our Lord and Father, and with it we curse human beings who have been made in God's likeness."
James 3:8, 9

II Come get your elephant!" These were the words that echoed down the hospital corridor on the maternity ward. The nurse on duty was calling my mother, citing that her baby was too large to bring to her. My mother said I was very fat when I was born. Maybe my mother's attending nurse was tired, had a bad day or just really felt that I was too heavy for her to carry. My mother very slowly, very carefully and painfully made her way from her hospital bed to the nursery to get her baby to feed her.

The nurse was fired; but her words, "Come get your elephant!" resonated with my mother and remained with me for over 40 years! Surely my mother did not tell me that story to make me feel bad. She still felt hurt. She always looked a little forlorn when she gave the account. The nurse demonstrated that she had no regard for my mother or her child.

Let's be very careful about what we say. We can encourage or discourage others, build up or break down with our mouths. If it hurts, it can damage a person for a long time; and if it helps, it can be a blessing forever. Be a blessing. Speak a kind word to someone today.

Reverend Brenda Smalls-Robinson

KEEP UP THE GOOD WORK

"Being confident of this very thing, that He who has begun a good work in you will complete it until the day of Jesus Christ."
Philippians 1:6

G od wants us to have confidence in His word, confidence in the relationship that we have with Him. This relationship is knitted through prayer and faith. There is a phrase that says, "prayer is the key and faith unlocks the door." Which means, prayer is the first step, but faith opens the doors to God's blessings. The good work Paul is talking about is salvation, and salvation is free through the grace of God. The good work is the word of God. We have confidence that God is a keeper through Jesus Christ. We keep up the good work by studying God's word and applying it to our lives and the lives we may come in contact with.

2 Timothy 2:15 *"Work hard so you can present yourself to God and receive His approval. Be a good worker, one who does not need to be ashamed and who correctly explains the word of truth."*

Ephesians 2:10 *"For we are God's masterpiece. He has created us anew in Christ Jesus, so we can do the good things He planned for us long ago."*

Reverend Graylan Richardson

Jesus Loves You So Very Much

"What shall we then say to these things? If GOD
be for us, who can be against us?"
Romans 8:31

GOD will never give up on you. Yes, you were created in His image and likeness. Yes, you are fearfully and wonderfully made by the Creator himself. In the eyes of God, He sees us as His precious children. We are honorable to Him, and HE loves us. The love of GOD continually transcends from heaven to earth and from earth to heaven. When JESUS ascended to the Father, He loved us so much that He didn't leave us alone. He left us the Comforter, which is the Holy Spirit **(John: 14:16).**

I was a sinner, destined for HELL, but GOD commended His love toward us. In all that, while we were yet sinners, CHRIST died for you and me **(Romans 5:8).** Remember, JESUS loves us this I know, for the BIBLE tells us so. *"For GOD so loved the world that He gave His only begotten Son (John 3:14)."*

JESUS is always at the door of our hearts. He is knocking and wants to come into our lives and become the LORD of our lives. Today, will you stop and listen to the voice of our **LORD AND SAVIOR JESUS CHRIST?**

HE LOVES EACH AND EVERY ONE OF US SO VERY MUCH!

Evangelist Arthur Gaddist

JUSTICE: WITHOUT JESUS THERE IS NO JUSTICE

"He is the Rock; His work is perfect. For all His work is perfect. For all His ways are justice. A God of Truth and without injustice; Righteous and upright is He."
Deuteronomy 32:4

The phrase "In God We Trust" has been on our currency since 1957. It came into existence because a group of strong Christians felt that a nation going through a painful costly war needed a constant reminder of God and His provision. The concept was made into law, becoming an intricate part of our national history. We need to be reminded today about our loyalty to God and His Word. We need to be reminded to trust Him. Jesus at the beginning, life in between and eternity at the end of our earthly time.

Justice begins with a "J." J stands for Jesus, the Author and the Finisher of our faith. The foundation that we can depend on. The foundation that can and has stood the test of time.

Reverend Dr. Brenda Joyce Stallings

THE LORD HEARD YOUR PRAYERS

"I sought the Lord, and He answered me; He
delivered me from all my fears."
Psalm 34:4

H ave you ever prayed, and it seemed as if God did not hear your prayer because you did not get the immediate response to your prayer request at your expected time? The Psalmist of this text makes a declaration that the Lord answers prayers. We are told by Him in this text that *"I sought the Lord, and He answered me; He delivered me from my fears* (Ps. 34:4, NIV)."

This text reminds us that God not only hears us but responds to the cries of His people. Our prayers do not fall on deaf ears. Yes, God hears us! I know this to be true because He has heard my cry prayers. God knows what is going on in all of our lives. Guess what? God hears your cry, and He will answer you if you would just trust Him to do it in His time. Remember, God's timing is not the same as ours. If you do not give up and quit, you will see your prayers answered.

David reminds us that God is still answering prayers even today. His Word is true, and He can be trusted to do just what He said He would do concerning us. God promises to hear and answer our prayers, and when He does, we too will be able to testify of the goodness of the Lord by saying, "I sought the Lord, and He heard and answered me." God hears you! He will answer you because He is true to His Word.

Minister Debra Aiken

GOD'S PLAN FOR ME

"Be very careful, then, how you live—not as unwise but as wise, 16
making the most of every opportunity, because the days are evil
There is a call to keep your "standards high, act
wisely, and do good whenever you can."
Ephesians 5:15-16

How might I do this you ask? God's wonderful plan for our life is that we repent, believe in Him, and fight sin through His power. God's wonderful plan for our life is sober-mindedness, sexual purity, and that we "walk not as unwise, but wise, making the most of our time because the day is evil."

Yes, your life may not be going the way you what it to go but it is going exactly as God wants it to go. You can rest in this fact. All you need to do is ask God, what is His plan for your life?

How then might I approach this task?
Listen for clue through the Holy Spirit.
Be patient in the wait for an answer
Follow God's will and ways, not yours.
Surrender your agenda.
Learn about yourself.
Pay attention to the circumstances in your life.

Minister Janet Williams-Johnson

_____
_____
_____
_____
_____
_____
_____
_____
_____
_____
_____
_____
_____
_____

Our Heavenly Father

*"The Spirit you received brought about your adoption
to sonship. And by Him we cry, 'Abba, Father."*
Romans 8:15

T he concept of God as our Heavenly Father is a powerful reminder of His deep love and care for us. Throughout the Bible, God reveals Himself as a Father who desires a close, personal relationship with His children. In Matthew 6:9, Jesus teaches us to pray, *"Our Father in heaven, hallowed be your name."* This is an invitation to approach God with reverence, but also with the confidence of being His beloved children.

In Romans 8:15, Paul writes, *"The Spirit you received brought about your adoption to sonship. And by Him we cry, 'Abba, Father.'"* Through Christ, we are adopted into God's family. The word "Abba" is an intimate term, similar to saying "Daddy." It shows that our relationship with God is not distant or formal, but personal and close.

Our Heavenly Father is also our provider and protector. In Matthew 7:9-11, Jesus says, *"Which of you, if your Son asks for bread, will give Him a stone? If you, then, though you are evil, know how to give good gifts to your children, how much more will your Father in heaven give good gifts to those who ask Him!"* This reminds us that God knows our needs and wants to give us good things.

When we face challenges, we can always trust our Heavenly Father to be there for us — guiding, comforting, and loving us through every season of life.

Minister Sonja Pinckney Rhodes

_____
_____
_____
_____
_____
_____
_____
_____
_____
_____
_____
_____

The Shepherd's Voice Matters Most

"Today, if you hear His voice, do not harden your hearts."
Psalm 95:7-8

We are constantly surrounded by noise—social media, opinions, expectations. Yet, only the Shepherd's voice leads to life. Tuning in takes discipline, but the clarity it brings is worthwhile.

Journal Prompt: What voices compete for your attention, and how can you better hear God's voice today?

Reverend Dr. Byron L. Benton
Senior Pastor

DECEMBER

"For unto us a child is born, unto us a Son is given: and the government shall be upon His shoulder: and His name shall be called Wonderful, Counsellor, The mighty God, The everlasting Father, The Prince of Peace."

Isaiah 9:6

FROM BLESSING RECEIVER TO BROKENNESS RESTORER

"Share your bread with the hungry..."
Isaiah 58:7

G od doesn't bless us merely to fill us, but to flow through us. We're called to be restorers—to mend what's broken, offer what's needed, and love as we've been loved.

Journal Prompt: Who or what around you needs restoration? How might God be calling you to help?

Reverend Dr. Byron L. Benton
Senior Pastor

THE NAMELESS DISCIPLE

"Jesus answered and said to her, "If you knew the gift of God, and who it is who says to you, 'Give Me a drink,' you would have asked Him, and He would have given you living water."
John 4:10

Her name? Unknown. Unrecorded. We know she had a name once. But time, with its cruel hand, had erased it, leaving behind only a nameless woman, a vessel carrying the weight of a life lived. The woman, when she met Jesus, paused, her bucket suspended in silence as her eyes met His. In that moment, a connection was forged, a silent understanding that transcended words. He spoke of living water, a spring that quenched thirst forever. She, with a touch of skepticism, inquired about the practicalities of fetching such water. Their dialogue delved deeper, into the heart of faith, the nature of worship, and the longing for something more.

This woman was not merely a nameless figure, but a soul yearning for redemption. Yet, in Jesus' eyes, she was not defined by her mistakes but by her capacity for change. Others may not have known all of her story, but Jesus knew her history. He saw her not as a Samaritan woman, but as a daughter of Abraham, a child of God. He saw her potential, her strength, her capacity to love. In that moment, she became more than a name; she became a symbol of hope, a testament to the transformative power of grace.

Minister Rosalyn Brown

GOD IS DOING A NEW THING

"For I am about to do something new. See, I have already
begun! Do you not see it? I will make a pathway through
the wilderness. I will create rivers in the dry wasteland."
Isaiah 43:19

God is at work, transforming your life in ways you can't always see with natural eyes. He's not waiting to begin—He's already started. In the barren, broken places, He's creating something new. Where there's been hurt, He's bringing healing. Where there's been sorrow, joy is rising. The dry deserts of your life are about to flow with rivers of His provision and grace. The wilderness moments, where you felt lost and unsure, are now pathways being made clear by His power. But can you see it? To recognize what God is doing, you must look with eyes of faith, not fear. Don't focus on what isn't—focus on what is becoming. Trust that His plan is unfolding, even when it feels slow. Walk by faith, believing that the new thing He's doing is for your good and His glory. Today's Declaration: I declare that God is making pathways in my wilderness and rivers in my wastelands. I will walk by faith and embrace the new thing He is doing in my life. Today's Challenge: Take a moment to thank God for the new thing He's already begun. Write down one area of your life where you need to trust Him to bring transformation, and declare His promises over it. Watch as He makes a way where there seemed to be no way.

Reverend Randy Adkins Jr.

_____
_____
_____
_____
_____
_____
_____
_____
_____
_____
_____
_____
_____

My God, In Whom I Trust

"I will say of the Lord, He is my refuge and my
fortress, my God, in whom I trust."
Psalm 91:2

M ay you uncover a profound sense of hope and reassurance in your life. This message highlights the importance of recognizing that even during the most uncertain and challenging times, there exists a steadfast and reliable source of protection and strength that you can turn to. By placing your trust in God, you open yourself to finding peace amidst the turbulent storms of life.

Understand that you are not alone; you are supported and shielded by a power greater than yourself. Embracing faith, whether it takes the form of spiritual beliefs, personal convictions, or a sense of community, can serve as a solid foundation for resilience and comfort. This faith not only provides a sense of security but also nurtures hope for a brighter future, encouraging you to navigate life's difficulties with courage and confidence. Allow this belief to guide you, knowing that with it, you can confront challenges and emerge stronger on the other side.

Reverend Ocie Gay

God Wants To Use You

"God has given each of you a gift from His great variety
of spiritual gifts. Use them well to serve one another."
Peter 4:10

G od has given all His children spiritual gifts. He has a purpose and a path that He has set for you. You have got to be unwavering in using the God-given gift of which you have been anointed. You have got to be determined to use your God-given gift. You have to be committed to using your God-given gift. Your gift may be sharing what Jesus has done for you. Your gift may be loving others. Your gift may be giving grace or not judging others. Whatever your gift, you must be committed to using it and going wherever God takes you. God wants you to use what He has given you. You and your gift are essential to the body of Christ. When you use your gift, you bring glory to God. Trust that God has given you the strength and the ability to use your God-given gift. Will you begin using your gift today, or must you continue using it again?

Reverend L. Michelle Mitchell

_____
_____
_____
_____
_____
_____
_____
_____
_____
_____
_____
_____
_____
_____
_____
_____
_____
_____
_____
_____
_____

Do Angels Really Exist?

"Be not forgetful to entertain strangers: for
thereby some have entertained angels."
Hebrews 13:2

Yes, **Angels** do exist on the earth, to fight against Satan and His demons, and to protect the children of God. In **Psalms 91:11,** God gave the **Angels** charge over us and to keep us in all our ways. Remember when it seemed like your world was falling? You are having problems with your job, husband, and children. Our fight is not against flesh and blood but against Satan and His demons **(Eph. 6:12).**

When Mary was conceived with a child, she was perplexed. Joseph, her soon-to-be-husband wanted to put her away privately. God dispatched Gabriel, the messenger who stands in God's presence **(Luke 1:19).** Mary was told by Gabriel that she would conceive a Son and His name would be called Jesus. He who will save the people from their sins.

Yes, Angels do exist to minister to God's people. All Christians are heirs to Abraham, Isaac, and Jacob. All the promises in the Bible belong to us. Angels are called to minister to believers. **Hebrews. 1:14** states, *"Are they, not all ministering spirits, sent forth to minister for them who shall be heirs of salvation."* **Angels** are waiting at the throne for God to do His will ministering to His people. Remember, *"Satan comes to steal, kill, and destroy, but Jesus came that we might have life more abundantly* **(John 10:10)."**

Remember, Angels do exist!!

Psalms 103:21 - *"Bless ye the Lord, all ye His host (ANGELS) ministries of His that do His pleasure."*

Minister Arthur Gaddist

_____
_____
_____
_____
_____
_____
_____
_____
_____
_____
_____

MIND REGULATOR

"So I find this law at work: Although I want to do good, evil is right there with me. For in my inner being I delight in God's law; 23 but I see another law at work in me, waging war against the law of my mind and making me a prisoner of the law of sin at work within me. What a wretched man I am!"
Romans 7:21-25

Have you ever experienced another law attempting to take control of you? It is waging war against the law of your mind and making you a prisoner of the law. Sin is at work in your mind. What size is your T-shirt? Paul said another law or principle is at work in the members of your body. You haven't acted out those negative thoughts, but your mind, your mind is playing out the movie. Soon, you assign yourself as the leading actor in the motion picture. You begin to look for others to help you cast the movie.

Like King Ahad, he desired to own what belonged to another man: Naboth's vineyard which was an inheritance passed down to Him from His ancestors. Evil disguises itself in an unrighteous plot and plan to take what doesn't belong to it. You are in need of a "mind regulator." Someone that is in control to direct your thinking.

Minister Janet Williams

FINDING REST IN GOD

"The Lord is my shepherd; I lack nothing. He makes me lie down in green pastures; He leads me beside quiet waters."
Psalm 23:1-2

I n today's busy world, it's easy to feel overwhelmed and exhausted. Between school, work, and everything else, we can sometimes feel like we're running on empty. But God invites us to find rest in Him, a rest that goes beyond physical sleep and restores our hearts and minds.

In Matthew 11:28-30, Jesus says, *"Come to me, all you who are weary and burdened, and I will give you rest. Take my yoke upon you and learn from me, for I am gentle and humble in heart, and you will find rest for your souls."* This is an invitation from Jesus to lay down our worries, stress, and burdens at His feet. He promises that when we come to Him, we will find rest that satisfies our deepest needs.

Rest isn't just about taking a break from work—it's about finding peace in God's presence. Psalm 23:1-2 says, *"The Lord is my shepherd; I lack nothing. He makes me lie down in green pastures; He leads me beside quiet waters."* God offers us peace and tranquility, guiding us to stillness where we can find true refreshment.

When we rest in God, we trust that He is in control. Instead of carrying the weight of the world on our shoulders, we can rely on His strength and grace. So, when life feels overwhelming, remember that true rest is found in God alone.

Minister Sonja Pinckney Rhodes

IMITATOR OF CHRIST

"Therefore, be imitators of God, as beloved children. 2
And walk in love, as Christ loved us and gave Himself
up for us, a fragrant offering and sacrifice to God."
Ephesians 5:1

Recently, I experienced a bit of discomfort and decided to change my gold shoes while in the car. In the rush, I accidentally left one foot of shoe behind as I headed into the house. The following day, I spotted that lone gold shoe and was reminded of the story of Cinderella. Just like her, who left her slipper behind as she fled the ball, our personal interactions often leave behind traces of who we are. This was the only piece of evidence the prince found that connected Him to the memory of the evening they shared.

Each encounter allows us to leave a piece of ourselves with others. What do you leave behind? This question takes on profound significance if you are a disciple of Christ. What message does your spirit, words, and actions convey about your identity? Are you leaving evidence that you are an ambassador of God's Kingdom, with the love of your Heavenly Father reflected in your life? Wherever we go, it's essential that we consistently embody and share the qualities of our Father.

Reverend Valarie Pritchard

HOPE THAT REACHES BEYOND THE PAST

*"By faith the prostitute Rahab, because she welcomed the
spies, was not killed with those who were disobedient."*
Hebrews 11:31

Rahab wasn't the likely choice. A woman with a tarnished past,
known by her profession, living in a city destined for destruction.
And yet — she had heard of the God of Israel. Not just rumors,
but reports of His power, His might, and His faithfulness to His people.

Something stirred in her. She didn't know the full story. She didn't
have a spotless record. But she had *hope* — and she acted on it.

When Rahab hid the Israelite spies in Joshua 2, she risked her life
based on a hope in a God she barely knew. That hope was counted as
faith — and that faith saved her, and her entire household. Not only was
her life spared, but her name was honored among the faithful (Hebrews
11:31), and she became part of the lineage of Jesus Christ (Matthew 1:5).

Rahab reminds us that hope can cover what shame tries to expose.
It can break generational cycles, rewrite reputations, and shelter those
closest to us.

You don't have to have it all figured out. You don't need a perfect
history. You just need enough hope to believe God is who He says He
is — and to act on it. That kind of hope is holy. That kind of hope saves.

*What area of your life feels disqualified by your past — and how might hope
in God rewrite that story if you dared to trust Him like Rahab did?*

Minister Rhulaunda Donald

GOD IS

"God is our refuge and strength, a very present help in trouble...
The Lord of hosts is with us; the God of Jacob is our fortress."
Psalm 46: 1, 7

L ife brings many blessings, but there are times when we face challenges such as loss and trauma, which can trigger feelings of loneliness and isolation. Emotions like hopelessness, worthlessness, sadness, and helplessness can seep into our daily lives, leading to moments filled with tears. Perhaps you have experienced or witnessed traumatic events that evoke these feelings. The psalmist in chapter 46 points to a source of solace: God is always ready to help in times of despair. *"The Lord of Heaven's Armies is here among us; the God of Israel is our fortress (verse 11)."* Remember, our Father in Heaven is omnipresent; He is present everywhere at the same time and can truly understand our feelings. How do I know this? He experienced sadness and wept surrounding the death of Lazarus, as noted in John 11:35. Rest assured, His love will reach you and provide comfort, regardless of your physical location, emotional state, or mindset. God embodies joy and strength. He has promised never to leave us, remaining faithful to His promises. His love serves as a constant source of comfort and strength. God Is!

Minister Dr. Lucretia D. Wilson

_____
_____
_____
_____
_____
_____
_____
_____
_____
_____
_____
_____
_____
_____

GRIEVING FOR LOVED ONES

"Blessed are those who mourn, For they shall be comforted."
Matthew 5:4

My husband, John, and I had always planned to retire in South Carolina. We envisioned spending our days visiting family, sightseeing, golfing, and staying active in church. At the time, my parents were spiritual leaders at Mount Moriah Missionary Baptist Church in North Charleston, and I was pastoring my second church in Queens, N.Y. We hadn't set a retirement date, but in 2007, the Lord blessed us to purchase a retirement home in Goose Creek, S.C. — paid in full. My parents joined us at the closing, beaming with pride that we wouldn't have a mortgage.

We decided to move to South Carolina in 2015, but none of our plans came to fruition. Shortly after relocating, Mommy became ill and soon transitioned to be with the Lord. I was heartbroken — no more shopping trips to her favorite store, Hamrick's, and so much more. While grieving her loss, my husband John, my rock, transitioned on September 21, 2016. I was devastated. Then, to deepen the pain, my only daughter transitioned on December 23, 2022. Each loss shook me to my core and changed my life forever.

I was comforted by God the Holy Spirit. He put people in my life that prayed with me and walked with me during this grief process. I went to the Grief Share Ministry which helped me tremendously. God's plan includes both sorrows and joys. As a believer, I don't mourn as an unbeliever but I do mourn.

Reverend Dr. Brenda Joyce Stallings

FORGIVE YOURSELF

*"For all have sinned and fallen short of the glory of God. Being
justified freely by His grace through the redemption that is
in Christ Jesus. God set forth as a propitiation by His blood
through faith to demonstrate His righteousness, because of His
forbearance God had passed over the sins that were previously
committed. To demonstrate at present His righteousness, that He
might be just and the justifier of the one who has faith in Jesus."*
Romans 3:23-26: Romans 8:1-2

F or us to live our best life, we should learn to forgive ourselves, realize our faults, confess our sins to God and to ourselves, and move on. God can redeem the lost time and start us out on a new path. Jesus paid it all, to one time for all of us. Jesus went the cross one time; there is no need for Him to go to the cross again We need to learn to accept the price He paid for us, and live our lives according to the example He left us, being led and guided by His Spirit as He renews our mind. Trust Him.

Romans 8:1 says, *"There is therefore now no condemnation to those who are in Christ Jesus, who do not walk according to the flesh, but according to the spirit. V2. For the law of the spirit of life in Christ Jesus has made me free from the law of sin and death."*

Reverend Samuel Fennoy

_____
_____
_____
_____
_____
_____
_____
_____
_____
_____
_____
_____
_____
_____
_____
_____
_____
_____

REMEMBER TO SHOW AND REMIND OTHERS

"Now then, we are ambassadors for Christ, as though God were pleading through us: we implore you on Christ's behalf, be reconciled to God. For He made Him who knew no sin to be sin for us, that we might become the righteousness of God in Him."
2 Corinthians 5:20-21

"**W**hile Christ intercedes before the Father for us *(Romans 8:34)."* We represent Him, bringing the kingdom of God to those around us who do not know Him yet.

For some, we're the closest thing to God they'll experience all day/week/month/year ...

So let's go forth each day believing for grace to light the way for others.

Minister Wallace Hunter

A Life With No Regrets

"Hear me, Lord, and answer me, for I am poor and needy. Guard my life, for I am faithful to you; save your servant who trusts in you. You are my God; have mercy on me, Lord, for I call to you all day long. Bring Joy to your servant, Lord, for I put my trust in you."
Psalm 86: 1-4

The taste of regret is one that is bitter and often lingers on the mind for lengthy periods of time. I, for one, have had many regrets in life, such as the friends I chose to associate with, the people that I hurt, the many broken promises I wish that I had kept, and the precious times I chose to spend doing foolish things instead of spending them with loved ones. If we were to name all the regrets we had in life, I am sure there would be too many to name all of them. But there is a way that all our regrets can be made right, and that way is when we form a relationship with Jesus Christ and recognize Him as our Lord and Savior. This is a decision that assures us no matter what choices we make in life, God is there to make sure that the truth of the Gospel of Jesus Christ guides us toward His perfect will. So, take courage in obeying His word knowing that all sins and trespasses are forgiven. Yes, we may still have to live with the consequences of our choices, but we can rest assured the guilt, shame, and regret of these decisions are not ours to carry because Jesus Christ has set us free.

Minister Tristan Simmons

THE LORD IS OUR STRENGTH

"Lord's strength is made perfect in weakness."
Corinthians 12:9

The strength of the Lord is a powerful, unyielding force that sustains us through every challenge and uplifts us when we feel weak. It is not a strength we can summon on our own, but a divine power that flows from God, made available to all who trust in Him. When we feel overwhelmed or exhausted, His strength becomes our anchor, reminding us that we do not face life's struggles alone.

In times of difficulty, it's easy to rely on our own abilities, but true strength is found in surrendering to God. As the Bible says, "The Lord is my strength and my shield" (Psalm 28:7). When we lean on His strength, we tap into a source that never runs dry. It empowers us to rise above our circumstances, to persevere when things seem impossible, and to face each day with courage and hope.

God's strength is not just about enduring hardship — it also equips us to move forward, to achieve things we never thought possible, and to step into the future with faith. It is a strength that turns weakness into opportunity, despair into hope, and fear into boldness.

So, when you feel weary or discouraged, remember that the Lord's strength is made perfect in weakness (2 Corinthians 12:9). His power will carry you through, and His presence will strengthen your heart. Trust in Him, and let His mighty strength be the foundation upon which you stand. You are more than capable, because His strength is always with you.

Minister Sonja Pinckney Rhodes

What Is In A Name

"Therefore, God also has highly exalted Him and given Him the name, which is above every name, that at the name of Jesus every knee should bow, of those in heaven, and of those on earth, and of those under the earth, and that every tongue should confess that Jesus Christ is Lord, to the glory of God the Father."
Philippians 2:9-11

There is no name or title given to man that is greater than Jesus our Savior. Titles and labels hold power, but true influence comes from action, not self-proclamation. Aspiring to greatness requires humility and a dedication to service, not empty pronouncements. True impact resonates through deeds, not words, shaping legacies that echo far beyond any given name. Let your actions speak louder than any self-bestowed title, for authenticity shines brighter than any artificial crown. Strive to embody the qualities you admire, and your influence will naturally follow. Here are some takeaways:

Humility and service: True leaders are humble and dedicated to serving others. They don't seek recognition or praise, but rather focus on making a positive impact.

Actions over words: Words are empty without action. It's our deeds, not our self-proclamations, that truly matter.

Authenticity: Authenticity is key to genuine influence. People are drawn to those who have genuine influence. People are drawn to those who are genuine and sincere, not those who put on a facade.

Minister Rosalyn Brown

_____

_____

_____

_____

_____

_____

_____

_____

_____

_____

_____

_____

Radical Love Requires A Radical Choice

"Choose life... loving the Lord your God."
Deuteronomy 30:19-20

God never forces love—He invites it, and you choose each day how to respond. Will you love radically, forgive courageously, and serve faithfully? The upside-down kingdom is built through small, daily choices.

Journal Prompt: What radical choice can you make today that reflects God's love?

Reverend Dr. Byron L. Benton
Senior Pastor

_____
_____
_____
_____
_____
_____
_____
_____
_____
_____
_____
_____
_____
_____
_____
_____
_____
_____
_____
_____
_____
_____
_____
_____
_____
_____
_____

"Now to Him who is able to do immeasurably more than all we ask or imagine, according to His power that is at work within us, to Him be glory in the Church and in Christ Jesus throughout all generations, forever and ever! Amen."

NOTES

NOTES

NOTES

CONTRIBUTING AUTHORS

Reverend Dr. Byron L. Benton
Senior Pastor

Reverend Randy Adkins, Jr.

Minister Debra Aiken

Reverend Leonard Bailey

Minister Carmen S. Bowman

Minister Rosalyn Brown

Reverend Larry Curry

Minister Rhulaunda Donald

Reverend Samuel Fennoy

Evangelist Arthur Gaddist

Reverend Ocie Gay

Dr. Pamela Gay

Minister Wallace Hunter

Reverend Gloria Lightfoot

Reverend Michelle Mitchell

Minister Anna Montgomery

Reverend Valarie Pritchard

Dr. Da'rrell Ravenell

Minister Sonja Pinckney Rhodes

Reverend Graylan Richardson

Minister Kon Robinson

Reverend Thomas Robinson

Minister Dr. Nathalina Rogers-Tolbert

Reverend Julette M. Scott

Minister Tristan Simmons

Reverend Brenda Smalls-Robinson

Reverend Dr. Brenda Joyce Stallings

Minister Janet Williams-Johnson

Minister Dr. Lucretia D. Wilson

MOUNT MORIAH MISSIONARY BAPTIST CHURCH
A BEACON OF HOPE AND HEALING

Mount Moriah Missionary Baptist Church stands as a beacon of hope and healing; a Christ-centered community devoted to spiritual renewal, theological depth, and transformative service. Rooted in the teachings of Jesus Christ and guided by the enduring truth of Scripture, we are committed to cultivating spiritual growth in individuals, families, and the broader community. Our faith finds expression through passionate worship, intentional fellowship, compassionate outreach, and a steadfast pursuit of justice and mercy.

As a congregation, we believe that every life has divine significance. At Mount Moriah, spiritual formation is not simply a church activity; it is a sacred journey. Through dynamic worship and the study of God's Word, we provide a nurturing environment where disciples are formed, hearts are healed, and purpose is awakened.

Our outreach reflects the heart of Christ, engaging in efforts that restore dignity, address systemic inequities, and extend the love of God to all people. We take seriously the call to be repairers of the breach, responding to the brokenness of our world with tangible acts of grace, advocacy, and reconciliation. Empowered by the Holy Spirit, we aim to embody the healing presence of Christ and make a lasting, redemptive impact in the lives of those we serve.

Flowing from this call, our vision is to positively impact every individual, family, and community through the healing and transformative power found in Jesus Christ, our Lord and Savior. Grounded in this vision, our mission is to love God, love people, and make disciples for Jesus Christ through worship, fellowship, education, and outreach. These guiding principles shape all that we do as we strive to be a church that radiates the love of Christ and builds a brighter, more hopeful future for all.

SYNOPSIS

T his inspiring book is a journey through the profound truth that hope in God is not just a comforting thought but a powerful anchor for our souls. Life often brings uncertainty, challenges, and even suffering, but hope in God remains steadfast. It is a hope rooted not in temporary circumstances, but in the unchanging character of God and His promises.

We've seen that true hope comes from understanding who God is—faithful, loving, and sovereign. This hope is secured through the resurrection of Jesus Christ, which guarantees us eternal life and a future beyond our current struggles. As 1 Peter 1:3 tells us, through Christ's resurrection, we've been given "a living hope" that cannot be shaken.

Hope in God also empowers us to persevere in difficult times. The Bible teaches that suffering produces endurance, endurance builds character, and character strengthens our hope (Romans 5:3-4). Every challenge we face can deepen our trust in God, refining our faith and making us more like Christ.

Through the penned words in this book, we have learned that hope in God is not just an abstract idea, but a living, active force in our daily lives. It shapes our perspective, strengthens our resolve, and fuels our joy, no matter the season. As we hold fast to the hope we have in God, we can move forward with confidence, knowing that He is faithful and that our ultimate hope—eternal life with Him—is secure.

Written and Compiled by:
Minister Sonja Pinckney Rhodes
Associate Minister, Mount Moriah Missionary Baptist Church

www.ingramcontent.com/pod-product-compliance
Lightning Source LLC
Chambersburg PA
CBHW051511120626
46551CB00012B/879